SPEAKING
IN
TONGUES

Enjoying Intimacy With God Through Tongues and Interpretation

Matthew & Kathleen Schwab
With Chris McKinney

CALLED WRITERS
CHRISTIAN PUBLISHING

Contents

CHRIS'S STORY

Foreword:
Tears of Intimacy

by Chris McKinney

When I agreed to read and evaluate this book, I had no idea what I was getting into. I thought it would be interesting, of course, and that my evaluation might be helpful. I certainly wasn't expecting any kind of life change, but that's exactly what I got.

But before we dive into that, let me back up and tell you a little about myself. I am an Executive Editor for *GODSPEED Magazine*. I also write for various other Christian magazines, websites, and ministries. I received Christ as Savior when I was ten years old, but the last seven years have been very powerful for me, as I have walked more closely with the Lord than ever before. In many ways, these years have been like a spiritual bootcamp.

After receiving the baptism of the Holy Spirit in 2016, the next year of my life was very interesting to say the least. God showed me my spiritual gifts, including my primary gifting and calling. I don't think I would have discovered this without the baptism of the Holy Spirit. I may not even have the spiritual gifts and anointing I have now. In other words, I'm not sure there would have been a whole lot worth discovering.

But I thank God that I did receive an infilling of His Spirit. What followed was a thrilling and exhilarating time of discovery and development. It was very exciting, so much so that even as a writer, I struggle to find words that will do it justice. It was amazing and wonderful, that's for sure.

I'm now in a second exhilarating, thrilling, and wonderful season of life, and it's all because of this book! The first item worth noting was that as I got a little ways into the book, God gave me the perfect answer to a question I'd had for a very long time about a certain phenomenon that is sometimes witnessed in charismatic circles.

My family occasionally visited charismatic churches growing up, but we mostly went to non-charismatic churches. I struggled to understand much of what I witnessed in charismatic circles, and to be honest, I even mocked some of it in my younger years. Even in recent years, I didn't understand a lot of the things that are common in Pentecostal or otherwise Spirit-filled services. But one by one, God lovingly and patiently alleviated my concerns and doubts.

By the time this manuscript was put into my hands, the issue of control was really the only outstanding question I still had about common charismatic practices. I had really struggled with the concept that people would appear to be somewhat "out of control" when being moved by the Holy Spirit because one of the fruits of the Spirit is self-control. Until reading Kathleen's testimony, I had never seen a good answer to the questions I had about the issue of control.

That answer alone made me realize God was working through the book—that there was an anointing on it. But it didn't stop there. I was sending notes to the authors such as, *"I've learned several very important things"* and *"Continuing to read and make notes... very insightful!"*

As I progressed through the book, I began to realize God was using this book for more than just increasing my knowledge and understanding. Here's the end of a note I wrote to the authors as I progressed through Kathleen's section:

"Most importantly, the book is touching me spiritually and making me say, 'Lord, I think there are still things about You that I'm missing. I want more of You.'"

As I continued to ask for more, He continued to lead me and put desires in my heart. I realized that a gift which would allow me to interpret my own tongue is right there in Scripture, but I had always glossed over it for some reason. Now I was understanding that this was a real, active, and available gift, and that I could ask for it.

One morning, around the time I was getting close to the end of Kathleen's section, I got up and the first thing I did that morning after reading John Chapter 17 was pray: *"Lord, I want the gift of interpretation. I yield my tongue to you, and I ask you to give me the interpretation of what I prayed."*

He gave it to me! Here is how it reads:

> *"Bring people together by the power of Your Holy Spirit and transform their minds and hearts. Stay close to us as we stay close to You. Bless our endeavors to bring You glory and transform the world. Give us more of Your joy as we fulfill the calling You have for us to spread the Gospel and transform the world."*

When I read it back that first day, I was thinking about my wife, myself, Matthew, and Kathleen. I was thinking that the prayer was really about this book, and the broader calling God has for all of us. But as I look at it now, I wonder if that prayer was for the entire Body of Christ. I wondered even that day if the prayer had been influenced by John 17, and specifically the way Jesus prays in that chapter. He prays to the Father for unity in the Body of Christ so that the "world may believe that you have sent me."

Shortly after receiving that first interpretation, I came to a section in the book where Matthew describes the various experiences of receiving an interpretation, and my experience matched closely with his descriptions. I felt a strong sense of confirmation, and I was excited that I'd received a new spiritual gift! But it didn't stop there.

The next morning, I prayed again in tongues and asked for the interpretation. What I received this time was life-changing:

"You don't know how much I long for you.

Because of my faith, I'm never alone. I always want to be closer to You, but I don't always know that myself. I always want to be with You in so many ways, but I get distracted and busy. I love You."

I cried for the next 10-15 minutes after reading the interpretation. I wouldn't call them tears of joy or of sadness; I could only think to call them tears of intimacy.

None of the ideas or themes represented in the prayer were on my conscious mind at all before I prayed. I was actually thinking about my relationships and interactions with other people, since I had just read Philippians 2 before praying.

I try to be personal and intimate with God in my "normal" prayer time (praying with my understanding), but at the time when this happened, I had mostly been approaching prayer like a business meeting: "Okay, God, here is what I can do for You today, and I need You to do these things for me..."

I was amazed to see the difference in the way my spirit man prays versus the way I normally pray with my conscious mind. It was so much more intimate and childlike. One thing I can say for sure is that God's Spirit touched me deeply as I read the interpretation.

However, there was something about this second interpretation that really confused me. I didn't understand the first line because God knows everything. How could I tell God that there was something He didn't know? For a long time, I thought I had made an interpretation 'error' with the first word—that it should have been 'I' instead of 'you.' More than two months later, I concluded that the first line was actually God telling me that I didn't realize how much *He* longs to have more time and intimacy *with me*, and the rest of the message was my spirit man's response to Him.

After coming to that realization, I pondered that statement for a while—that God longs for me. I've always heard preachers say things like, "God doesn't need anything" so it perplexed me a little, because we would normally think of this kind of statement as the expression of an emotional need. After pondering it for a week or two, I somehow came across this Scripture in a "random" morning reading:

*"Is not Ephraim my dear son, the child in whom I delight? Though I often speak against him, I still remember him. **Therefore my heart yearns for him;** I have great compassion for him,' declares the LORD."*

– JEREMIAH 31:20 (NIV)

Getting back to the morning of that second interpretation, I thought I was done after praying the prayer I shared earlier. But then I felt the Holy Spirit gently nudging me and saying, "We don't have to be done. Keep going." What followed was a full handwritten page of interpretation, which came a sentence or two at a time. It was very intimate and personal to me, and it did have some personal revelation in it (I share portions of it in my story at the end of this book).

There is now a new spiritual gift in my life that I am using daily. This gift increases my intimacy with the Lord. The benefits didn't stop there. More learning and growth was in store for me as I progressed through the book. I continued to gain more understanding and knowledge as God continued to work in my life. Matthew and Kathleen have written a book that God can use to open up some of the "mystery" surrounding tongues, and in so doing, to deeply touch other people's lives and strengthen their relationship with God. I have no doubt about that, because I have experienced it.

I have more to share, but that will have to wait for a later section. I don't want to unduly influence anyone else's experience by sharing all of the details about my own experience here in the Foreword. Instead, I just wanted to share enough to whet your appetite and help you get a sense of the wonderful adventure that lies ahead for those who are hungry and thirsty for more of God's Spirit in their lives.

We now invite you to read and have your own experience with the Lord—one that He has undoubtedly tailor-made just for you. Be encouraged that God shares your desire for more closeness and intimacy, and remember, *His heart yearns for you.*

INTRODUCTION

by Kathleen Schwab

In 2012, I became convinced that very little guidance existed in the Christian world for speaking in tongues. I was exploring the idea of doing a blog, and I wanted to write about topics of personal interest that weren't already covered exhaustively online. When I decided I might want to write about speaking in tongues, I poked around to see what cyberspace already had to offer. No point in being redundant.

One thing I discovered is that over the past few decades scientists have studied speaking in tongues from both a linguistic angle and a neurological angle. Linguists analyzed recordings of people speaking in tongues, and neurologists ran tests on the brains of tongue speakers. Thousands of research hours, as well as thousands of test subjects, went into providing a modern, scientific perspective. But I found very little writing from a Christian perspective on the scientific research, how it reflects Christians' experiences, and whether it offers insights for believers in their own exercise of spiritual gifts.

As far as the Christian world goes, I found that the internet has plenty of debates about whether speaking in tongues is a legitimate practice for a Christian, including Bible studies for both sides. But I did not find first-person narratives about subjects like:

- How speaking in tongues impacts the life of a believer
- How it changes a Christian's spiritual experience
- How it doesn't change a Christian's spiritual experience
- How speaking in tongues feels emotionally
- What place it finds over the long term in a person's relationship with God
- After practicing the gift of tongues for a while, what is the next step?

I spent roughly a year researching and thinking about what I would write. During that time, I came to believe there wasn't much teaching available to guide Christians about how and why to pray in tongues. The biggest question that gets addressed is whether speaking in tongues is an acceptable practice for today, but once the decision is made for yay or nay, not much else is said.

At least that was my experience when I researched the topic years ago. The situation reminded me of the complaints I heard from new mothers about birth education: "They spent so much time educating me about pregnancy and labor, but

I hardly heard anything about being a mother. It was like everybody forgot that was the main point!"

As I researched, I started mentioning my project to friends. During that time, I would often hear people say, "I used to speak in tongues." The statement often sounded wistful. No one had a clear reason for stopping, just a shrug and, "I don't know. I just don't anymore." This led me to wonder why people dropped speaking in tongues. I wondered if anything could be done to help them access the gift in a way that would make them want to stick with it, because it was making their lives richer.

I can't claim to have definitive answers about this, but I think many Christians abandon speaking in tongues as a spiritual practice because it remains too much of a mystery for too long. People aren't sure quite what to do with it, or how it integrates with the rest of life. What exactly is the purpose of praying in tongues (or "praying in the Spirit" as Scripture sometimes refers to it)? Why speak in tongues rather than spend the same amount of time praying in one's native language, or Bible reading, or service? Once the excitement of a new experience wears off, why continue?

This book is an attempt to fill in these gaps. The first section reflects on over thirty years of experience with speaking in tongues, and the results in my Christian walk. Over and over again, I found that the recent scientific research shed light on my own experiences and instincts about speaking in tongues, so I'll be sharing about that along the way.

What Comes Next?

This first section answers the first five questions in the previously given list. The last question, "What comes next?"

is addressed in the section by my husband Matthew, who writes about developing the gift of interpretation. I have not developed the gift of interpretation myself.

While I know many people who speak in tongues, or who spoke in tongues at some point in their lives, I know only a few who interpret. Matthew's section of the book, as well as Chris's Story, should prove helpful in that area. In his section, Matthew also delves into what Scripture has to say about the spiritual gifts, and how to use them in church life. My section is more personal. It's more about how speaking in tongues fits into the life of an individual believer.

Matthew began to move in the gift of interpretation about a decade ago, but I didn't seek it for myself. I was settled into a comfortable way of using my gifting, and I didn't feel the urge to develop the gift of interpretation. Hopefully I can grow in this area going forward.

Part One:

TONGUES

THE GIFT OF SPEAKING IN TONGUES

by Kathleen Schwab

S peaking in tongues is a spiritual practice through which a
believer speaks words that he or she doesn't understand.
These words are used to commune and communicate
with God. Speaking in tongues is recorded in the Book of
Acts, taught in the epistles, and was even prophesied in Jesus'
statement from Mark 16:17 that those who believe in Him
would "speak with new tongues."

Speaking in tongues is practiced by many Christians today.
Pew Research Center estimated in 2011 that there were roughly
584 million Christians worldwide who believe in the baptism
of the Holy Spirit, and "engage in practices such as speaking in
tongues."[1]

I have been speaking in tongues for over thirty years.
During that time, I haven't exercised the gift every single day,
but I have exercised it most days. I write from the perspective of
someone deeply familiar with the practice, but in a private way.

My History of Speaking in Tongues

I haven't talked very much with others about speaking in tongues, even with those I am closest to. A few years ago my then-teenage son asked me, "What is this thing—speaking in tongues?" because he had read about it in one of Paul's letters from the New Testament. I gave him a quick rundown of the New Testament history and theory behind the practice. Then I added that I began speaking in tongues in college, and do so regularly now. He looked perplexed. "Why don't I know this?" he asked.

I found myself a little surprised he didn't know. I think of us as close, and this is an integral part of my inner life, so why didn't he know? I didn't realize until then that while I may speak in tongues often, I can go for years without talking to anyone about it.

Tongues has been an inner journey for me. It is deeply personal. I began to speak in tongues during my junior year of college. It was the late 1980s, and I belonged to a small church of the sort which at that time called itself 'charismatic.' Nearly everyone in the church spoke in tongues, so I began my journey in a supportive environment. As far as I know, everyone who wanted to speak in tongues did so without much effort.

Some people would lay hands on the person who wanted to receive this gift, and in fairly short order the person would begin. As far as I can remember, nearly everyone who sought the gift received it. Perhaps because it all happened easily and naturally, my friends and I viewed it as just another aspect of Christian life. The gift of tongues was cool and being college students, we liked cool stuff. It existed in the continuum of cool things we were excited about in our Christian lives.

This is how it began for me. The first thing I did was ask a couple of my college friends to describe how they received the gift of tongues. I approached each person in a one on one situation so that I would get each individual story without filtering. I was impressed that although each had unique details, they were more alike than different—and everyone was enthusiastic about this gift adding depth to their Christian lives. While fully understanding the experience before it actually happens may be impossible, I wanted to hear from my peers that this gift was worth pursuing.

After I was sure I wanted to proceed, I thought about where and how I should begin. I realize now that I was naive about this, but I assumed that I would probably start speaking in tongues whenever I decided to. Why wouldn't I just be able to plan it out? The idea of starting in my dorm room by myself was unappealing; after church on Sunday seemed much better. So during church that week I told the pastor's wife I was seeking the gift of tongues, and a group of people laid hands on me and began praying.

I turned my attention to God and waited. Nothing seemed to be happening. This was maybe three to five minutes after everyone began praying. Then one of the women put her head close to mine, and said, "You're doing it!"

I replied, "I don't think so." I felt doubtful. I wasn't sure how to gauge this.

"Weren't you praying just now?" she asked.

"Yes," I answered.

She was getting a big smile on her face. "And was it in English?" she added.

"No," I concluded, surprised. I suppose I needed someone to walk me through what had just happened.

She said, "That's what this gift is. You are talking to God, but not in English—in your own language that God gives you. Pray in English or in tongues, whichever you want."

So I began the process of finding where it fit. One of the first things I discovered was that tongues was a great tool for helping me focus. Starting off morning prayer time with some tongues helped me settle into the moment. I liked getting to Sunday service early anyway and having some time to set my mind on worshiping God. Praying in tongues was great for times like that, when I just wanted to get my heart and mind focused on Him.

When I was praying in a large group, I would pray quietly in tongues during the gaps and pauses that naturally happen. It kept my mind from wandering. By praying in tongues, I could remain in God's presence, while at the same time staying aware of the corporate experience of worship.

Another early reaction I had to tongues was how unimpressive it sounded. Anyone overhearing it would probably just think you were saying random syllables, if they spared it any thought at all. "It doesn't sound like anything" was the comment from one church friend. We both laughed a little and shook our heads.

Though other people's experiences might be different, another surprise for me was how little I actually felt. I didn't exactly expect the clouds to part with a peal of thunder, but I thought I would feel some sense of elation, or something like that. Instead, no particular emotion was attached to the experience. But still, I continued exploring this new ability.

Following my junior year of college in 1989, I signed on with a ministry which sent college and seminary students to lead informal worship services in the national parks during the summer break. They assigned me to Smoky Mountain National Park, so I spent the summer in a small cabin. It was in a wilderness area where I got to plan worship services for campers, work a day job for the park service, and spend time praying. I had been speaking in tongues only a few months at this point, and was still finding my way.

Often that summer I felt a desire to speak in tongues for extended periods, continuing on much longer than I might have initially planned. I was in the perfect setting for this type of prolonged communing with God. I had plenty of privacy, and once I was off work there was little demand on my time. I walked in the woods and let the tongues have free rein; it seemed to well up and push its way out, like an underground river suddenly finding its way to the surface. I believe that Jesus' words from John 7:38-39 were being fulfilled in my life during that time.

"'He who believes in Me, as the Scripture has said, out of his heart will flow rivers of living water.' But this He spoke concerning the Spirit, whom those believing in Him would receive;"

– JOHN 7:38-39A (NKJV)

My footsteps fell into the rhythm of this free-flowing river. Alone in the wilderness I didn't have to think of interrupting or disturbing anyone—I was free with only myself and God.

What happened during all those sessions? I didn't keep track of time, nor have any agenda other than to let it happen. As I write this, that summer is 30 years in the past, and my sense is that during this time a foundation was laid down in my spiritual life that I have been building on ever since.

In Ephesians 3:16, Paul talks about how the Holy Spirit strengthens the inner man. In my experience, praying in tongues did exactly that; it built up some inner part of me that connects to God. This is my sense of what happened with me internally. It also fits with the 20th verse of Jude, which says:

"But you, beloved, building yourselves up on your most holy faith, praying in the Holy Spirit."

– JUDE 20 (NKJV)

This is potentially a huge benefit for anyone who is struggling against their flesh. It makes sense that when you strengthen the inner man, you can more easily overcome the flesh. After all, Paul says in Galatians:

"I say then: Walk in the Spirit, and you shall not fulfill the lust of the flesh. For the flesh lusts against the Spirit, and the Spirit against the flesh; and these

are contrary to one another, so that you do not do the things that you wish."

– GALATIANS 5:16-17 (NKJV)

If I want my spirit to have more power and influence over my mind and body, it makes sense that I should want to do things that strengthen my spirit (or "inner man") and keep me more connected to God's Spirit. This is one of the major benefits of praying in tongues, and it's actually backed up by scientific research.

When I read the book *How God Changes Your Brain*, published in 2009 by Andrew Newberg, MD, I discovered that a number of spiritual exercises change the brains of practitioners. Newburg studied Pentecostals praying in tongues, but he also studied Franciscan nuns praying, and Buddhist monks meditating. Dr. Newberg found that tongue speakers' experience was unique in the sense that it activated different areas of the brain. He also discovered that all of these practices changed the brain in measurable ways, strengthening different centers depending on the practice. The results were clinically measurable, and they increased over time.

This mirrors my experience during that long-ago summer. The time I spent speaking in tongues felt like exercising muscles I had just discovered. I was like a person who had never been athletic, and then found a sport that suited my physique perfectly. It felt good; it felt right; it felt like something I was made to do. It felt like I was becoming the person I was meant to be. This experience, again, fits with what we find in Scripture. For example, 1 Corinthians 14:4 tells us that "He who speaks in a tongue edifies himself." (NKJV) The Greek word translated there as "edify" can also be translated "build up" as it is in the ESV.

In the years since then, speaking in tongues has settled into a regular place in my life as a Christian. I often do it when I am alone. Normal prayer that includes prayer requests, or even talking over my life with God, requires focused attention.

For praying over requests or for a full conversational prayer, I need to set apart dedicated time and focus. If possible, I like to have pen and paper to write down impressions from God, because I've learned how poor my memory can be about these. I like to have a Bible handy in case a Scripture comes to mind and I want to check context. I also enjoy prayer journaling. This means that I need a little space, and isn't always practical for me when I'm out of the house, or when my hands are busy.

Speaking in tongues, on the other hand, can be done while sorting laundry, picking up clutter, and so on. It can fill your life. It can be employed in the middle of corporate worship during natural lulls and pauses, or as a way of quietly praying along with someone who is offering a public prayer in a larger group. I do this very quietly, enunciating under my breath, sometimes silently in order to avoid disturbing the group.

Sometimes I sing in tongues, following the melody of the worship song being played. When the song is unfamiliar, I'm even more likely to do this. I think it is because following a new song takes some focus, and employing tongues helps me maintain my focus on God.

A factor in my worship behavior may be that I am quite unmusical. I'm probably tone-deaf, and I have a singing voice no one but God would want to hear. In daily life I have almost no interest in listening to music, a fact that puzzles some people. Employing tongues during musical worship may be simply a way for me to operate in a venue (language) which works well for me, rather than one (music) which has never held much interest.

Tongues is as <u>unobtrusive</u> a gift as can be imagined. It is simple, just like many other powerful spiritual practices. As in my case, no one else even has to know you are practicing it.

WHAT IS THE
EXPERIENCE LIKE?

In my research, I read quite a few articles about speaking in tongues written by people who have never experienced it themselves, and no matter how scholarly, they often strike a distorted note. They just don't know what it is like. They've observed other people doing it but they haven't experienced it, and there is all the difference in the world between the two. I could compare it to seeing a marriage counselor who has never been married themselves. Dr. Smith may be well-read, compassionate, insightful, and licensed in marriage and family therapy, but at some point he just doesn't know what he is talking about. He doesn't have a full, experiential understanding of all the dynamics of marriage.

One misconception is that people who are speaking in tongues are out of it—perhaps less mentally present. Some years before I began speaking in tongues, one person described it to me, "And then they get on such a *wavelength with God* that this other language comes out," giving the idea that tongue speakers get a bit into another dimension. The web article "Speaking in Tongues: a Neural Snapshot," published on the site BrainBlogger in 2010, says, "It has commonly been considered a form of ecstatic trance."

While I can see why people might think this, nothing is farther from the truth, in my experience. The issue of awareness, and the connected issue of control, are not so simple. We can often misinterpret other people's worship experiences and draw wrong conclusions about what we're seeing. The following story may shed some light.

WORSHIP NIGHT WITH THE
TWENTY-SOMETHINGS

S ome time ago, I went to a healing service at a friend's invitation. Since developing chronic pain I tend to avoid crowds, because even a little light jostling can significantly impact my pain level. During this service, as the room got more crowded than I expected—and the empty space around me disappeared—I began to feel anxious. I thought sitting in the front row would give me a buffer of personal space, but then the traveling ministry team set up chairs to the side of the front row, and I ended up nearly knee-to-knee with a group of twenty-somethings—a situation my rickety body normally tries to avoid.

The music started, and the twenty-somethings began to respond in ways that will be familiar to anyone who has attended a charismatic, Pentecostal, or Spirit-filled service. They were jumping, shaking, moving with fast jerks, and occasionally diving prone onto the carpeted floor. I tried not to cross the bridge from anxiety to fear. More than once I had ended up with my pain level spiraling out of control after getting shouldered at a sporting event, or stumbled into at the mall.

Suddenly, the young woman nearest me jackknifed. She had been standing upright, and swiftly, as though someone had pushed her powerfully, she folded in half at the waist. Most people can laugh off a collision with another body, but not me. I thought she was going to slam down right into my lap, but instead she caught herself lightly with two fingers on my knee. She put almost no weight on me. She lifted her face and smiled reassuringly. I smiled back. She came as close as could be, and she moved with force, yet I saw that she was perfectly aware of me. She could tell, I was sure, that I was nervous about my physical space.

The rest of the service was the same: the twenty-somethings continued their communion with God complete with its physical expression, but not one of them so much as brushed up against me. They surely had a part of their attention taken up in this ecstatic communion with God, but I felt safer with them—as distracted as they may have appeared—than I have felt in any other crowd. They were more in control of themselves and more aware of their surroundings than the average mall crowd.

Like the young men and women at that service, when I speak in tongues, I am perfectly aware of my surroundings. I am focusing on communing with God, but my sight, hearing, and all of my other physical senses continue to work just fine.

THE IMPACT OF TONGUES
ON THE BELIEVER'S LIFE

How the practice of praying in tongues intersects with the rest of Christian life is another area where I hear and read statements by non-tongue speakers that don't match my experience. While doing a bit of internet research, I came across an article originally published in a professional journal for theologians. The writer had this to say about speaking in tongues: "The faith of glossolalists is based on their inner emotional voice."[2]

This is not my experience, nor have I ever heard any of my friends speak about their tongues experience that way. To the extent that I've talked it over with others, everyone seems to agree that tongues isn't particularly emotional, nor is one's faith in God dependent on feelings caused by tongues. I can see how an outside observer might assume that people speaking in tongues must be experiencing heightened emotions, but that has never been the case for me.

The writer in this particular article meant his comment as a criticism of the effect of speaking in tongues on the overall Christian life. He thought people who spoke in tongues depended on their feelings, and the practice of speaking in tongues confirmed them in this view. Then, when life got tough as it inevitably does, and the feelings weren't flowing, they tended to walk away from Christianity.

As I read over the article, I couldn't help getting the impression that the writer just plain didn't like tongues. He didn't seem to like people doing it, and therefore fastened on to any comments from tongue speakers which confirmed his opinion that it was all going to end badly.

In my own experience, I've never seen tongues harm anyone's Christian life. I know people who spoke in tongues at one time, and now seem to have walked away from their faith, but speaking in tongues was not the issue. I've read a few accounts of Christians who spoke in tongues at one point in their lives and have stopped, but have continued as Christians. My experience is that tongues has greatly strengthened my Christian life. It appears to have done the same for many of my fellow Christians, although the effect is far from universal. Tongues is no panacea.

ALPHA STATE

As I read scientific studies about tongues, I began to analyze my own behavior in light of the new information I was receiving. I realized I only speak in tongues in environments where I feel completely safe: in my favorite corner of the living room before my family comes down in the morning, alone in my prayer room, or in a group service with people I trust. One aspect of the research shed some light on this for me.

Several online articles noted that brain imaging of people speaking in tongues showed a decrease of activity in the area of the brain associated with control. In a *New York Times* article titled "A Neuroscientific Look at Speaking in Tongues," one test subject described her experience: "You're not really out of control. But you have no control over what's happening."[3]

Maybe another way to say it would be that you retain control in the sense that you can stop it at any time. You're able to turn it on or off as willing partner with the Holy Spirit. But when it's on, you aren't really the one generating the words. It feels more like something flowing out of you.

This dichotomy describes my experience with tongues, and also explains to me why I have always been so selective about where I speak in tongues. Some who study brain function refer to a time called the "alpha state" when brain activity associated with control slows down or diminishes. During this time, the person is more suggestible, more impressionable. Though I had never put it into words, I knew that while speaking in tongues my guard would be down. I would be more vulnerable. I allowed this to happen only in situations where I felt secure.

This also leads me to reflect on one possibility of how tongues may operate in the Christian life. Given that it ushers in an alpha state, tongues is the perfect way to begin a time of personal prayer. It also helps to more fully participate in corporate worship. In the Christian life, a believer is constantly seeking to follow God more closely, figure out what God wants them to do in the situations they face, and experience a sense of God's presence. Christians also talk about yielding to God in various ways, and submitting our will to His.

Here is a tool which puts you into a state where you are more open to God's influence! Use it at carefully chosen times, and you are likely to come more and more under God's influence, while at the same time remaining fully yourself. To my mind, this is a lovely picture of the dance between God and the individual believer.

1970s LINGUISTIC RESEARCH

The most extensive and well-known linguistic work on speaking in tongues remains the 1972 book *Tongues of Men and Angels*, a 300-page doorstopper of a book based on ten years of research among Pentecostals. Renowned linguist William Samarin of the University of Toronto brought both a linguistic and an anthropological lens to his research on speaking in tongues, and conducted himself with great respect towards the people he studied.

Samarin taped thousands of people speaking in tongues in both private and public settings, and included subjects from diverse ethnic backgrounds. Samarin included subjects with different native languages so that he could determine how the language a person spoke in everyday life affected their tongue speaking.

Samarin concluded that speaking in tongues, although it resembles language, is not a language. Here are some of his reasons:

- Speakers use phonemes from a language they speak themselves, never any sounds from languages they do not speak
- Tongues lacks internal grammatical structure
- All humans use language to communicate meaning—speaking in tongues does not communicate meaning in any measurable way

After extensive research, Samarin described speaking in tongues as "a meaningless but phonetically structured human utterance believed by the speaker to be a real language but bearing no systematic resemblance to any natural language, living or dead."

I read only parts of Samarin's writings, but I was impressed by the thoughtfulness he brought to his research. He respected the tongue speakers who volunteered in his studies, and was genuinely interested in their experiences. The same could not be said for several of his linguistic colleagues who sometimes analyzed samples. They made little to no attempt to hide their disdain for the Pentecostals and the practice of speaking in tongues.

I suspect Samarin's attitude of taking his subject seriously from a scientific point of view resulted in the large number of volunteers who participated in his study: thousands of people volunteered as test subjects. On the flip side, I think that one of the things which limited his research was the rigid science of the 1970s. People were not viewed holistically at that time.

Today we accept the idea that experience and emotion have a profound influence on the physical body, and that spirituality is connected to all aspects of a person.

However, in the 1970s the view was drastically simplified, to the point where I think doctors and scientists had only a shallow understanding of the complexity of human beings. The family was not yet understood as an intricate and interconnected system, PTSD symptoms of such traumatized individuals as battlefield soldiers were poorly understood, and the reality of intergenerational trauma was so far outside the paradigm that no one in the establishment even recognized its existence.

In his book _The Body Remembers,_ psychotherapist Basil Vanderhof writes that in the 1970s mental health professionals believed that childhood sexual abuse had little to no impact on a person's adult life. In the 21st century we take the profound destructive impact of childhood physical and sexual abuse for granted. Our society has come a long way in the past four decades in understanding how complex human beings are.

When I look at Samarin's conclusions about tongue speaking, I see a siloed view. His statement that "speaking in tongues does not communicate meaning in any measurable way" is one I think most, if not all, of his test subjects would have disagreed with. They believe they are communicating with God. Of course, how could this be measured in a lab? As 1 Corinthians 2:14 says:

"But the natural man does not receive the things of the Spirit of God, for they are foolishness to him; nor can he know them, because they are spiritually discerned."

– 1 CORINTHIANS 2:14 (NKJV)

I've talked about speaking in tongues being a part of the inner life of a Christian—a highly personal connection between the individual and God. To open that communication to any other person would diminish it: the privacy is an integral part of the experience. The intimacy of an exchange between one person and an infinite God is charged with deep meaning. Of course, this also cannot be measured in a lab.

My husband recently had an experience which confirms the sometimes private nature of praying in tongues. He was in a ride-share situation with a group of strangers, and he heard a woman speaking under her breath in tongues. Since my husband has the gift of interpretation, he silently began the process of interpreting her tongue: almost immediately he felt a wall go up, and he sensed that God was telling him, "*Her tongue is for private communion with Me. It is not meant for you to interpret.*"

This is a case where language was not supposed to communicate meaning to another person, but only to God. Samarin's statement that "speaking in tongues does not communicate meaning in any measurable way" assumes that a person uses language to communicate *only to other human beings*. However, we know that tongues are designed for communication with God.

LESS CAN BE MORE

This brings to mind a case of less language leading to a greater depth of communication. Richard Wurmbrand, who founded Voice of the Martyrs, was persecuted by communist authorities in Romania when the state was officially trying to eliminate all religion. In various testimonies (especially in an essay Wurmbrand wrote which was published in a 1981 compilation book called *My Path of Prayer*), Wurmbrand described how he was drugged and tortured during his imprisonment, and his memory suffered to the point where he could remember only the first two words of the Lord's Prayer. So he went with what he had, and repeated *"Our Father"* over and over.

He explains that those two words encompassed more and more profound meaning for him as time went on. Conditions in the prison did not improve, and eventually Wurmbrand lost the ability to remember *any words* from the Lord's Prayer.

At first he was frightened, feeling he had lost his ability to communicate with God, but then he decided that God had heard the prayer from him many times already, and so he simply prayed that God would count that he had said it again that day.

A profound peace followed this decision. Then things became even worse, and Wurmbrand lost his ability to form words at all—he thought for about two years. He wrote that he believed God counted as prayer the beating of a devoted heart, and seeing his experience this way brought about once more a deep sense of peace and trust in God.

The above story turns Samarin's assumption that more complexity will equal more meaning on its head: the less complexity Richard Wurmbrand found himself capable of linguistically, the deeper his communion with God became.

WHAT IS LANGUAGE?

What is language, and how does it overlap with communication? How many words and how much grammatical structure do you need for communication? How much for self-expression? I think the following story sheds some light on these questions.

I went to visit a friend some years ago and brought my toddler daughter along. While my friend and I sat in her living room catching up, my daughter slowly wandered through the room, studying the many family photos on tabletops and shelves. First she walked around and looked, and then she began to delicately touch one fingertip to the glass of each picture, pointing to the face of a child. She went from table to windowsill to knickknack shelves, locating children (she ignored the adults in the pictures) and intoning softly, "Baby, bay – bee." She was absorbed in finding all the baby pictures in the room, and her voice took on a dreamy quality.

My friend and I both paused to watch this, and my friend said, "That's all the love you've given her... that's what you can hear in her voice." I think she was right: my daughter was summing up her own life experience in those two syllables. In the word "bay-bee," she was investing all of the feelings and events of her year and a half of life with Mommy, Daddy, and her big brother.

It was communication, but with no grammar, and only one word. How much can you communicate with one word? In my daughter's case, I think she communicated a lot. Of course, the meaning was rich for me because of my intimacy with her; at that point in her life we had hardly been apart at all. A stranger coming in with no context might have thought she was simply recognizing the difference between children's and adults' faces.

I think speaking in tongues can be like that. Many people who speak in tongues regularly are aware that it can be quite repetitive. Tongue speakers often have their own sounds and words that they will repeat over and over, sometimes for years.

Tongues has the effect of easing one into an alpha state—a state in which one is more open to God's influence—and that alone is one valuable aspect of it. But I think the meaning of a simple set of sounds spoken in tongues may be as rich as my daughter's "bay-bee." God hears us, and I believe we communicate much more to Him than the sounds themselves imply. No researcher, however, would be able to figure this out.

DANIEL AND THE
WRITING ON THE WALL

A story from Chapter 5 of the Book of Daniel has some interesting things to say about language and meaning. King Belshazzar, who was a descendant of Nebuchadnezzar, was having a feast. After drinking some wine, he was emboldened to completely disrespect God by bringing in the holy vessels from the temple, and using them along with his guests. Not only that, but he and his companions actually worshiped false gods while they drank from the holy vessels.

At that point, something supernatural showed up on the scene—a hand which wrote a mysterious series of words on the wall (this is the origin of our phrase, 'the writing is on the wall.')

Belshazzar was incredibly frightened, and called all of his wise men and diviners in to tell him the interpretation of the supernatural message. They could not give him any interpretation whatsoever, and that's where we pick up with the biblical text:

Then Daniel was brought in before the king. The king spoke, and said to Daniel, "Are you that Daniel who is one of the captives from Judah, whom my father the king brought from Judah? I have heard of you, that the Spirit of God is in you, and that light and understanding and excellent wisdom are found in you. Now the wise men, the astrologers, have been brought in before me, that they should read this writing and make known to me its interpretation, but they could not give the interpretation of the thing. And I have heard of you, that you can give interpretations and explain enigmas. Now if you can read the writing and make known to me its interpretation, you shall be clothed with purple and have a chain of gold around your neck, and shall be the third ruler in the kingdom."

Then Daniel answered, and said before the king, "Let your gifts be for yourself, and give your rewards to another; yet I will read the writing to the king, and make known to him the interpretation. O king, the Most High God gave Nebuchadnezzar your father a kingdom and majesty, glory and honor. And because of the majesty that He gave him, all peoples, nations, and languages trembled and feared before him. Whomever he wished, he executed; whomever he wished, he kept alive; whomever he wished, he set up; and whomever he wished, he put down. But when his heart was lifted up, and his spirit was hardened in pride, he was deposed from his kingly throne, and they took his glory from him. Then he was driven from the sons of men, his heart was made like the beasts, and his dwelling was with the wild donkeys. They fed him with grass like oxen, and his body was wet with the dew of heaven, till he knew that the Most High God rules in the kingdom of men, and appoints over it whomever He chooses.

"But you his son, Belshazzar, have not humbled your heart, although you knew all this. And you have lifted yourself up against the Lord of heaven. They have brought the vessels of His house before you, and you and your lords, your wives and your concubines, have drunk wine from them. And you have praised the gods of silver and gold, bronze and iron, wood and stone, which do not see or hear or know; and the God who holds your breath in His hand and owns all your ways, you have not glorified. Then the fingers of the hand were sent from Him, and this writing was written.

"And this is the inscription that was written:

MENE, MENE, TEKEL, UPHARSIN.

This is the interpretation of each word. MENE: God has numbered your kingdom, and finished it; TEKEL: You have been weighed in the balances, and found wanting; PERES: Your kingdom has been divided, and given to the Medes and Persians." Then Belshazzar gave the command, and they clothed Daniel with purple and put a chain of gold around his neck, and made a proclamation concerning him that he should be the third ruler in the kingdom.

That very night Belshazzar, king of the Chaldeans, was slain.

– DANIEL 5:13-30 (NKJV)

This story takes place during the Babylonian exile, about 500 years before Jesus and the events of the New Testament. Speaking in tongues was a term not used—as far as anyone knows—until Jesus' statement in Mark 16:17, that those who believe in Him would "speak with new tongues." So Daniel's experience with the writing on the wall is not a direct description of this gift. However, the story gives some insight into language, and how linguistic issues play a part in messages from God.

Given the way it is delivered, by a disembodied hand which leaves writing on a wall, everyone would agree that this is a supernatural message. The king sends for his wise men, and they all say that they cannot read the writing. Babylon conquered many other people groups, and, as they did with Israel, they normally brought the most promising of the educated class from their vassal states to serve the king. Most of the languages of the empire would have been represented among the wise men.

When the prophet Daniel comes in, he translates the message into the language of Israel, which at that time was Aramaic. Perhaps none of the other wise men knew the language of the Jews, or perhaps the wise men were afraid of angering the king with an incomplete answer. It's possible that someone recognized the words but couldn't put them into a coherent message, and therefore opted to stay quiet.

The message itself contains only three words, and does not have grammatical structure. Instead, the meaning depends on other information. To make sense out of this message, Daniel draws on his knowledge of recent history, the personalities and motivations of the previous and current kings, the nature of the God of Israel, and the surrounding military powers. A person would not have been able to come into the banqueting hall ignorant of all of these things, aand still be able to assemble the words into a meaningful message the way Daniel did. This particular message also uniquely leverages Daniel's life experiences.

Let's look at the message itself. On a literal level, these words are values in currency. The word *MENE* refers to a mina. *TEKEL* is a variant of shekel, and *PERES* (which is the singular form of *UPHARSIN*) is the value of half a mina. In ancient valuation a mina was worth about fifty shekels. So it could be said this way: "Fifty shekels, one shekel, twenty-five shekels." To Americanize it, you might say something like, "a silver dollar, a quarter, a fifty-cent piece" or "a Benjamin, a George Washington, a Lincoln."

To tease out the full meaning of this supernatural news bulletin, Daniel uses some plays on words. These names for currency have root words which have their own meanings, so Daniel explains that the writing also means numbered, weighed, and divided. The part about the kingdom being given to the Medes and the Persians involves yet another play on words: taking a bit of poetic license, the word *PERES* also sounds very similar to "Persians" (*pārās* in Hebrew/Aramaic).

As Daniel makes sense of this message from God, the word *PERES* does triple duty, and means half a mina, divided, and Persia. Daniel then goes on to explain how these three words together mean that the king has offended God so badly that Babylon is about to be conquered, divided, and given to the Medes and the Persians.

Daniel is elderly at this point, and his interpretation draws on a lifetime of experience living as an exile in Babylon. Chapter 4 of the Book of Daniel recounts the story of how the former king, Nebuchadnezzar, was specifically warned by Daniel to avoid offending God with arrogance, or he would suffer insanity. Nebuchadnezzar does not follow Daniel's advice and becomes a madman.

After Nebuchadnezzar recovers, he practices humility and acknowledges the power of God. Being Nebuchadnezzar's direct descendant, Belshazzar should have learned from this dramatic example, but instead the first thing we hear about Belshazzar is how he uses the sacred vessels from Israel's temple to drink wine at a banquet. Daniel says that this arrogance will cost Belshazzar the kingdom.

From this example, we find that a simple message can carry a great deal of meaning—if you know how to interpret it. Interpretation is possible when you are the person with the ability or experience to do so. Words can carry more than one meaning, and history adds another dimension.

SIMPLE AND COMPLEX TONGUES

W e've covered a lot of ground about how tongue speaking often sounds linguistically simple, but linguistically complex messages do happen. (For some people, like my husband, complex messages happen all the time. In Part Two of this book he shares about complex tongues, and how to interpret your own tongue.)

I think two distinct phenomena fall under the category of "speaking in tongues." In my anecdotal experience, this is also a common belief among practitioners, though I've never even seen it mentioned in any of the scientific literature. This leads me to think the research community is unaware of this aspect of speaking in tongues.

The first, "praying in tongues" is the type which can be practiced at will by an individual believer, and which is a highly personal and internal experience. My writing here is about my experience with that type of tongue. The second, a different type of "speaking in tongues" is a message in a tongue, often given to a group, delivered by an individual and often followed by an interpretation. However, there is some overlap in regard to the terminology. My husband notes that "all prayer is speaking, but not all speaking is prayer."

Some Bible teachers also see a distinction in Scripture similar to what I'm describing here.[4] They see a distinction between "praying in tongues" and "the gift of tongues" with the former being a personal prayer language available to all believers who have been filled or baptized with the Holy Spirit. It is used primarily in a devotional way.

The latter is understood by some as a spiritual gift that the Holy Spirit only distributes to select individuals as He sees fit. This "gift of tongues" is for the benefit of more than one person. It can be interpreted by someone with the gift of interpretation, for the purpose of edifying a group of believers.

Whichever terminology you prefer, it's clear from the Bible and from experience that there are two different things which happen in regard to the common operation of tongues. One is personal and private; it's just between the individual and God. The other is public—meant for at least one other person—and there should be an interpretation.

How do you tell the difference? Personally, I think there is some confusion about where the line falls between the two, even by people familiar with the practice of speaking in tongues.

I'll give an example. Some time ago my husband went to a prayer meeting. During open prayer, he received a message for the group in tongues and spoke it out. Now the interesting thing was that while my husband was speaking, no one in the group realized he was delivering a message in tongues.

Everyone was either looking down or had their eyes closed for prayer, and no one even recognized his voice.

This was a group of less than a dozen people who mostly knew my husband quite well. The group thought that one of the men present must be praying aloud in his native language, which none of them understood. Only when my husband followed his tongues message with an interpretation in English did the group realize what had happened.

Now these were people used to hearing others speak in tongues, and many of them practiced tongues regularly themselves. But in this case they didn't recognize it when they heard it. As my husband later told me (I wasn't present), the message he gave did not have repetitive syllables: it sounded more like someone speaking a foreign language, with many different sounds.

I think the messages in tongues which sound more like a full language are quite rare, and this is why researchers seem unaware of them. Christians themselves can even be caught off guard when they happen. These messages do not seem to be produced at will, the way the other sort of tongues can be.

Just one more example along these lines. A few years ago, Matthew and I were in a church service together when a young man stood up and shared his belief that speaking in tongues was an underutilized gift. He explained his concern that while many of us spoke in tongues, we seldom spoke out loud to the group as reported in the New Testament. Therefore, he wanted to give a message in tongues to the group, and hoped that an interpretation would follow.

So he began, and what followed was the highly repetitive sounds often heard by tongue speakers. Someone in the group stood up in short order and gave the following interpretation:

"Bless you, Lord. Bless, bless, I bless you, I bless you, Lord. Bless you, Lord." The young man's expression struck me as a mixture of happiness that an interpretation had come so quickly, and disappointment that the message was not more complex.

In my opinion, he had delivered a portion of tongues which was the personal prayer sort, the kind tongue speakers can produce whenever they want. This type of tongue often has a simple surface meaning, just as it sounds. But the complexity of this communication if spoken between the individual and God could be profound: "Bless you, Lord" has the potential to express the experience of a lifetime, the way "bay-bee" did for my daughter.

Before the Ancient of Days, even an elderly human is an infant being. Ask any parent of a child just learning to speak whether that communication is not rich and profound. Often parents understand their child's speech when it is unintelligible to anyone else. It may have no grammar and only a few words, but it is charged with the deep relationship between the child and their parents.

THE SCIENTIFIC
COMMUNITY AND COMPLEX
TONGUES

Until recently, the scientific community doesn't appear to have captured any of the complex tongues. I couldn't find anything about it in older literature. Samarin, who recorded hundreds of hours of tongue speaking in the 1970s, always wrote about how linguistically 'restricted' his samples were.

Samarin asked other linguists to listen to the tapes, and here is the response of William Welmes, a professor of African languages at the University of California at Los Angeles: *"And I must report without reservation that my sample does not sound like a language structurally. There can be no more than two contrasting vowel sounds, and a most peculiarly restricted set of consonant sounds; these combine into a very few syllable clusters which recur many times in various orders. The consonants and vowels do not all sound like English (the glossolaliac's* native language), but the intonation patterns are... completely American English." (Christianity Today, Nov. 8, 1963.)

In contrast, Dr. Andrew Newburg writes in his book, How God Changes Your Brain: "In 2003 I brought in members from a Pentecostal church and scanned them while they engaged in the practice of speaking in tongues. To those unfamiliar with this practice, it may sound like a foreign language or like babble, but I have heard renditions that reminded me of medieval Italian liturgies and ancient Assyrian poems."

The mention of liturgy and poetry indicates that the language sounded both organized and complex. At least to the researcher's ear, it sounded like rich oral traditions that people pass from generation to generation as important cultural legacies. Did scientists become better at studying tongues between the 1970s and the early 21st century such that they were able to record these samples? Or is something happening in the population of people who speak in tongues? Are they manifesting different, more complex languages and messages?

I can't answer that question, but perhaps it will be answered in the coming years.

Another interesting thing to come out of recent scientific research is the fact that when people speak in tongues, they do not seem to be generating the language themselves. According to the previously referenced article, "A Neuroscientific Look at Speaking in Tongues," published by the New York Times in 2006, "Researchers at the University of Pennsylvania took brain images of five women while they spoke in tongues and found that their frontal lobes—the thinking, willful part of the brain through which people control what they do—were relatively quiet, as were the language centers. The regions involved in maintaining self-consciousness were active."

This information describes my experience with speaking in tongues. I am conscious and aware, while at the same time I don't feel as though I am coming up with the sounds myself. I believe that the Holy Spirit is enabling the language to come forth as I yield my tongue to Him. As 1 Corinthians 14:2 says of the one speaking in tongues, "in the spirit he speaks mysteries." (NKJV) For me speaking in tongues results in an internal experience that is unlike anything else.

The research from the above article also found unique patterns of blood flow in the brain while a subject spoke in tongues. The scientists collected data while the subjects were engaged in other devotional activities such as singing gospel songs. They found that speaking in tongues resulted in a signature series of peaks and valleys not found through any other activities. It was another example of the scientific data confirming my internal sense of what I experience.

CONCLUSION

If I may, I'd like to share a personal opinion I have formed about the nature of tongues, but please understand that it is only my opinion. As I mentioned previously, speaking in tongues involves speaking "mysteries" (1 Corinthians 14:2 NKJV). I don't believe a complete and provable understanding of it is available in this world.

When we speak in tongues, I believe we are beginning to exercise the language we will speak in Heaven, when face to face with God. Possibly, this language may be different, or at least different in some respects, for every individual (see Revelation 2:17). For instance, we may all have different words we use to address God, shaped by our experience with Him.

I believe that this language is deeper than any terrestrial language ever could be, in that it is capable of expressing more complexity. I believe it's also capable of expressing things which are distinctly the experience, feeling, or thought of one individual. I think we will be able to communicate in our 'own' language more specifically as ourselves than we have ever been able to do in this life, all speaking common languages.

In Heaven we will have fewer barriers between ourselves and God. Likewise, we will have fewer barriers between ourselves and others, but I suspect we will also become more distinct, more individual than we ever were before (see 1 Corinthians 13:12). I think language will play a role in this. Each person will be capable of communicating things that no other person could. A person's individual language will be one vehicle for this.

Speaking in tongues may be the beginning of the language of the next life. Why so repetitive? We are babies in that life. We have begun it in only the most rudimentary way. Another reason I think this is I have been listening to myself while I speak in tongues.

Before, my practice was to take advantage of the alpha state benefits of tongues, and pay little attention to the sounds. But while mulling all these things over, I've started to become more aware of sounds. Very rarely, I've heard what seems to be a new word, even sometimes a whole new string of sounds.

This has invariably happened at times when I pushed myself out of my comfort zone spiritually, and did something I would rather not do for the chance to grow closer to God. I think I may have added a new word to my heavenly language. I don't know what the word means. It could be that I gained a new word by God's gift. It could also be that my language developed a little as part of a process which occurred as I pushed my spiritual boundaries. Maybe it was a combination of the two.

Again, these are my best guesses as to the nature of my experiences, but what I am sure of is that tongues has greatly enhanced and deepened my Christian life. I appreciate the research that has been done in the past few decades, though research can only reveal so much about a mystery like tongues. However, thinking about the research has helped me to analyze my experience, and to understand it better.

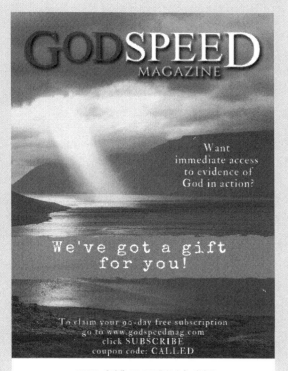

Do you enjoy reading about how God is moving and speaking and building His Kingdom on the earth? GODSPEED covers news that no one else covers! Here are a few of the recent stories covered exclusively by GODSPEED Magazine:

The Largest Mission Trip in History

1300 Native Israeli Jews Come to Christ
in a Single Meeting

11 Million People Saved Through
One Man's Divine Mission

1000 Days of Revival in Uganda

Holy Spirit Explosion in Kenya –
Thousands Saved, Baptized, and Filled

A National Day of Repentance for America

How a Baptismal Took Over DC's National
Mall

Recent Issue themes cover topics such as:

How God is Bringing Racial Healing
and Reconcilation

Miracle Healings

Revival

How God is Moving Through Technology

Infant Lives Matter

God's Fingerprints in Israel

Prophecy

How God is Acting on Behalf of Parents

Discounted Annual Subscription Offer:

Full of compelling interviews and Christ-centered coverage of God in action, GODSPEED is a magazine like no other. Get GODSPEED Magazine and be informed, encouraged, and inspired!

For a limited time only, readers who know they want the magazine can skip the free trial offer and take advantage of a $12 annual subscription (80% discount) by using the coupon code: **CALLED2020**

Just visit GODSPEEDMAG.COM and subscribe using the coupon code **CALLED2020** to take advantage of this very low-priced annual subscription.

Part Two:
INTERPRETATION

❧

Introducing the Interpretation of Tongues

by Matthew Schwab

With the topic of tongues well covered, let's turn our attention to the corresponding spiritual gift: the interpretation of tongues. Of the spiritual gifts listed in the New Testament, the interpretation of tongues seems to attract very little attention today compared to some of the other gifts. If you search for books or articles on the gifts of healing or prophecy, you are likely to find an excess. But if you try to find teaching about the interpretation of tongues, you will probably find relatively little.

This is not to say that the interpretation of tongues ought to be given equal weight with healing and prophecy. Healing was the gift Jesus used most commonly. Healing is also the gift—along with driving out demons—that Jesus' disciples used most often during Jesus' earthly ministry and on into the Book of Acts.

In contrast, the gifts of tongues and their interpretation did not even appear until after Jesus ascended. But even in the post-ascension world of tongues and interpretation, Paul admonishes us to seek the gift of prophecy far above the gift of tongues—though he also acknowledged that he spoke in tongues quite a bit.

All of that said, I would still argue that the interpretation of tongues should be given a greater emphasis among believers than it currently enjoys. What follows is my humble attempt to fill the gap regarding the interpretation of tongues.

INTERPRETATION,
NOT TRANSLATION

While I found very little teaching available on the topic of interpretation, perhaps the best teaching I did find came from Pastor Chuck Smith, the late minister who founded the Calvary Chapel movement. In his teaching, Pastor Smith underscored the difference between the word Scripture uses (interpretation) and what many of our minds hear instead (translation).[5] While all translations are interpretations of another language, not all interpretations could be properly called translations. Let me give you three different interpretations of the same hypothetical utterance— all of which would be quite legitimate.

1. As I listened to Jane's utterance, I felt her heart overflowing with praise to Jesus for what He is doing in our midst. I sensed how we all are experiencing the blessing of His sovereignty in the midst of these

challenges we have been discussing as a church community.

2. Lord Jesus, we praise You for being present here with us as we face these many challenges together in our church community. Your presence is a blessing. Thank You for Your sovereignty in this situation.

3. Lord Jesus—and in that name for Jesus, I felt how Jesus manifests His sovereignty in Jane's life and in our shared life as a church community. We praise You for being present—and in that word *present* I felt a deep sense of blessing in the Lord's presence among us, how He knows each of us intimately, and how He knows us as a church community, and will never leave us nor forsake us. We praise You for being present here with us as we face these many challenges together in our church community. Thank You, sovereign Lord Jesus—again Jane uttered that same name for Jesus that emphasized His sovereign Lordship and thanked Him for His sovereignty in our situation.

Each of the three interpretations above could be appropriate, depending upon the context in which the tongue and interpretation were given. Yet the three are clearly different. The first was a very general interpretation, the second was a translation, and the third was a more specific interpretation in which certain words were interpreted more deeply than a person would provide if merely translating.

The important thing to take away from this example is that when interpreting, you do not need to receive a word-for-word translation to meet the scriptural mandate to interpret.

The interpretation can be very general. Likewise, you can provide more detail than what would otherwise be provided in a mere translation, as the third example above demonstrated.

WHO SHOULD INTERPRET?

To properly answer the question of who should interpret a tongue in a public setting, we need to reconcile two seemingly contradictory statements Paul made.

*"But **the manifestation of the Spirit is given to each** one for the profit of all: for to one is given... different kinds of tongues, to another the interpretation of tongues."*

– 1 CORINTHIANS 12:7-10 (NKJV)

*"Therefore let **him who speaks in a tongue pray that he may interpret."***

– 1 CORINTHIANS 14:13 (NKJV)

At first glance, one almost wants to ask Paul, "Which one? Is it another, or is it the one who speaks?" But a closer read reveals that the passage from Chapter 12 simply provides a list of spiritual gifts, while Chapter 14 gives specific instruction. So the short answer to the question is that the one who speaks a tongue should also pray for an interpretation. Another insight we can glean is that when speaking a tongue in a public setting, the person who spoke the tongue may not be able to provide an interpretation. However, they should make the first attempt to provide an interpretation. If the speaker is unable to provide an interpretation, he or she should allow another to interpret, as described in 1 Corinthians 14:27.

What is the benefit of a separate person who has been given the spiritual gift of interpretation of tongues (as Paul mentions in 1 Corinthians 12)? Here are some possibilities. First, the gifted interpreter can serve to verify the speaker's own interpretation. Second, the gifted interpreter can interpret in the event the speaker is not able. Last, and perhaps most importantly, the gifted interpreter can provide more depth to the interpretation.

Remember, interpretation is not translation. Words, even in human languages, contain layers of meaning, which is why so many words exist with such similar meaning. As an example, consider the difference between the English words "beautiful" and "lovely." Or more importantly, consider the different names and titles for Jesus, the second person in the Trinity, which appear in Scripture: Jesus, Emmanuel, the Son of God, the Son of Man, and the Captain of the Lord's Army, to name just a few. All of those different terms add depth to our understanding of the person being described. Considering these examples, one can imagine the blessing of a deeper interpretation of a spoken tongue.

SIMPLE TONGUE OR COMPLEX TONGUE?

As discussed in Part One, when researchers began to look at the phenomenon of tongues and attempted to apply scientific analysis, they found a significant majority had very simple tongues. My observation has been that complex tongues are more common than what the researchers reported. In my experience, perhaps just a little less than half of believers speak in complex tongues. I do not know if this difference is a function of who volunteers for tongues research or the uniqueness of the circles in which I interact—or as Kathleen hypothesizes in Part One, whether the gift itself matures as the Body of Christ matures. Either way, many, many believers speak a simple tongue rather than a complex tongue.

As discussed, there is tremendous blessing uttering even one word to God whether in a known or an unknown tongue. After all, you are speaking to the God of the universe. And if uttering a tongue, you are speaking to the God of the universe who lovingly gave you a word to speak to Him.

What could that one word or short number of words mean? I have observed simple tongues are like the words a baby first learns to speak: a way to say mother, a way to say father, or a cry for help or for comfort. Regardless, the simple tongue speaks a very core, if not the core, aspect of the speaker's relationship with God. And regardless of the simplicity or complexity of your tongue, an interpretation will reveal a deep and highly relevant, Spirit-led overflow of the heart. If spoken before a group, it will be relevant to those present as well.

That said, a complex tongue speaks more—at least it speaks a more complex message. Among those who advocate seeking and exercising the gift of tongues, I have found little that encourages people to develop the language. Yet that is what every parent does when teaching a baby to speak. We should expect the Lord as our heavenly parent is willing and eager to help us develop our tongue. He will certainly do so if we seek Him.

For the individual believer, that person's current circumstances may determine whether growing the vocabulary of his or her tongue is a high priority at any given time. Again, it is worth noting that Paul places seeking to prophesy above seeking to speak in tongues (see 1 Corinthians 14:1-5). But at the same time, Jesus tells us that His yoke is easy and His burden is light. Adding to your tongue should not be a strain but an opportunity to grow closer to the Lord through this wonderful and mysterious gift.

DIFFERENT KINDS OF TONGUES

When Paul lists various spiritual gifts in 1 Corinthians 12, one is *different kinds of tongues*. Note Paul did not merely say "tongues" or even "different tongues," but different "kinds" of tongues. Often when reading Scriptures, I have come across something and wished the Lord had inspired Paul or one of the other writers to provide more detail. The reference to different kinds of tongues may fall into this category for many. While "different tongues" could easily be interpreted as multiple languages, the phrase "different kinds of tongues" appears to me to mean different categories of languages.

This suspicion is backed up just a little further on in Paul's first letter to the Corinthians when he refers to the tongues of men and the tongues of angels.

"Though I speak with the tongues of men and of angels, but have not love, I have become sounding brass or a clanging cymbal."

– 1 CORINTHIANS 13:1 (NKJV)

Here is a clear example of placing tongues into two separate categories. Other categories Kathleen and I can envision would include private prayer languages individual believers share with God, and prayer languages targeted toward a specific type of public prayer. Some Christian leaders have suggested even more categories than these. An international pastoral intern in our church community, Jens from Namibia, believes he has three distinct prayer languages: one when he prays to God on his own behalf, one when he prays to God on behalf of another, and one when he prays for healing.

This expanded view—that there is a gift of different kinds of tongues—adds weight to the concept that while all gifts are available to believers, there are special gifts. There could be a deeper or more powerful gift of healing, a deeper gift of prophecy, a deeper gift of interpretation, and a deeper gift of tongues called "different kinds of tongues."

THE TONGUES OF MEN AND
ALL FLESH

T he gift of tongues first appears in the second chapter of Acts. The story is interesting for several reasons.

"And they were all filled with the Holy Spirit and began to speak with other tongues, as the Spirit gave them utterance.

And there were dwelling in Jerusalem Jews, devout men, from every nation under heaven. And when this sound occurred, the multitude came together, and were confused, because everyone heard them speak in his own language. Then they were all amazed and marveled, saying to one another, "Look, are not all these who speak Galileans? And how is it that we hear, each in our own language in which we were born? Parthians and Medes and Elamites, those dwelling in Mesopotamia, Judea and Cappadocia, Pontus and Asia, Phrygia and Pamphylia, Egypt and the parts of Libya adjoining Cyrene, visitors from Rome, both Jews and proselytes, Cretans and Arabs—we hear them speaking in our own tongues the wonderful works of God." So they were all amazed and perplexed, saying to one another, "Whatever could this mean?"

Others mocking said, "They are full of new wine."

– ACTS 2:4-13 (NKJV)

This first instance of tongues in Scripture gives an example of believers speaking in unknown tongues of men, and speaking them publicly among unbelievers. If we cross reference Paul's instructions about not speaking in tongues in the presence of unbelievers, we can see that Acts 2 provides an exception. If one feels unction from the Holy Spirit to do so, one can indeed proceed.

I have heard various testimonies of believers approaching an unbeliever and explaining, "I think I'm supposed to say this to you." They then uttered a tongue and the unbeliever was able to understand, and even to tell the believer what the tongue meant. The tongue was an earthly language the speaker did not know, but the hearer did know.

Several hosts and guests on Christian television programming have also reported experiencing this in modern times. Perry Stone, who hosts the television show *Manna Fest*, testifies that both he and his father have experienced the blessing of speaking a tongue in the presence of someone who reported that their native language was being spoken.[6] Sid

Roth, who hosts the television show *It's Supernatural*, has also experienced this and has interviewed many guests who have likewise experienced it.[7] Such was effectively the case in the second chapter of Acts.

Or was that what happened in the second chapter of Acts? Not quite. The testimonies from the crowd *"how is it that we hear, each in our own language"* indicate that no matter what language the tongue was spoken in, the hearer heard his own native language. Each one was also simultaneously aware that individuals nearby with a different native tongue were hearing the words in their native tongue as well.

In other words, it was not followers of Christ who first interpreted by way of the Holy Spirit, but unbelievers. And what an impressive manifestation of the Holy Spirit's power! Somehow these unbelievers did not simply interpret the tongues in their mind but heard in their own language. Maybe this is what Paul refers to when he writes in 1 Corinthians 14:22, "Therefore tongues are for a sign, not to those who believe but to unbelievers." (NKJV) These people, who did not yet believe in Jesus, received a sign that day to demonstrate to them that what they were experiencing was from God. Still, some accepted the sign as being from God, and some unfortunately didn't.

Peter confirms the miracle of interpretation when he preaches from the Book of Joel:

"And it shall come to pass in the last days, says God, That I will pour out of My Spirit on all flesh."

– ACTS 2:17 (NKJV)

Without the benefit of Joel's exact wording, one might expect God would pour out His Spirit on all of His followers, or perhaps the house of Abraham. Instead it is *all flesh*. It includes believers and unbelievers, Jews and Gentiles, men and women, Greeks and barbarians. If you embrace Calvinist theology, it includes both the Elect and the Damned.

THE TONGUES
OF ANGELS

Why might God bestow the *tongues of angels* on some people? It does sound cool. You would be able to say, "My tongue is an angelic tongue." But what could be God's purpose in such a gifting? I think the answer lies in who (besides God and an interpreter) might understand what the utterance means. The angels understand. Isaiah reports a great chorus of angels singing to God in worship, "*Holy, Holy, Holy!*" With such a gifting, a believer could join or even lead the angels in prayer, worship, or both.

Conversely, the fallen angels understand. One of the leaders in our church community, Rena M. from California's San Lorenzo Valley, reported that while praying for a deliverance, she felt a strong unction to pray in tongues. No prayer seemed to be having any effect until she began to pray in this unknown language. The unclean spirit became very agitated. "*Don't speak that way! Stop saying that! Stop! Don't! No! Noooo!*" And then there was peace.

Her testimony regarding tongues is, "*I may not know exactly what I am praying. But the enemy certainly knows.*"

EXACTLY WHEN IS 'WHEN YOU GATHER'?

*"**H**ow is it then, brethren? Whenever you come together, each of you has a psalm, has a teaching, has a tongue, has a revelation, has an interpretation. Let all things be done for edification. If anyone speaks in a tongue, let there be two or at the most three, each in turn, and let one interpret. But if there is no interpreter, let him keep silent in church, and let him speak to himself and to God. Let two or three prophets speak, and let the others judge. But if anything is revealed to another who sits by, let the first keep silent. For you can all prophesy one by one, that all may learn and all may be encouraged. And the spirits of the prophets are subject to the prophets. For God is not the author of confusion but of peace, as in all the churches of the saints."*

— 1 CORINTHIANS 14:26-33 (NKJV)

To correctly apply Paul's instruction to a typical church community in America, some basic math is in order. Picture a Sunday morning meeting with 300 adults present. Imagine giving each person present the opportunity to share what he or she 'has' (as Paul puts it). There is a maximum of three tongues and three prophecies. There are also three interpretations, and at least three 'judgments' of the prophecies that were given. Everyone else has either a psalm, a teaching, or a revelation to share.

Imagine each person takes 90 seconds, including the transition time. 300 shares x 1.5 minutes each ÷ 60 minutes per hour = 7.5 hours. Not only would this be an excessively long meeting—and it would be prohibitively long if attempted in a megachurch—try imagining the actual value to those present. Would anyone even remember what was prayed, taught, or prophesied? This instruction of Paul's cannot be aimed at the sort of conventional Sunday morning meeting that is common in our culture. Everyone may "have" something, but it's not possible for *everyone* to share or provide what they have.

If not intended for the average church meeting, what "coming together" could Paul be referring to in his writing? I think the answer lies in Acts Chapter 2.

"So continuing daily with one accord in the temple, and breaking bread from house to house, they ate their food with gladness and simplicity of heart"

– ACTS 2:46 (NKJV)

While a large meeting like a conventional Sunday morning church service would not be a practical place to apply Paul's instruction, the size of a meeting that could occur at someone's house would be practical. Many church communities encourage and sponsor small meetings. These go by various names including potlucks, Bible studies, small groups, life groups, and home groups. We perhaps observe an example later in the Book of Acts.

 "On the next day we who were Paul's companions departed and came to Caesarea, and entered the house of Philip the evangelist, who was one of the seven, and stayed with him. Now this man had four virgin daughters who prophesied."

– ACTS 21:9-10 (NKJV)

In such smaller meetings, each participant—even a new believer—could bring something to share with the group. Tongues could be included, provided there was one present who could interpret.

Tongues and Interpretation in a Large Meeting

How can one include tongues in a large meeting? As mentioned above, *"each of you has"* applies only to meetings small enough for everyone to contribute meaningfully before the clock runs down. This is simply not the case in large meetings. As such, the first point here is that it is perfectly acceptable to exclude tongues from a large meeting.

"Therefore if the whole church comes together in one place, and all speak with tongues, and there come in those who are uninformed or unbelievers, will they not say that you are out of your mind?"

– 1 CORINTHIANS 14:23 (NKJV)

Paul teaches that there are two concerns regarding tongues when *the whole church comes together*. The first is regarding the *uninformed*. The second is regarding *unbelievers*.

Some people could be both *uninformed* and *unbelievers*. To address these two problems, leaders of a large meeting would need to explain what is happening, ensure that tongues and prophecies are limited in number, and ensure that each tongue is interpreted.

One could easily imagine how time-consuming such an explanation might be. And when should the explanation be given? Unless the doors of the church building are locked, anyone can come or go at any time. So, in theory the uninformed and unbelievers could miss the announcement and then come in during the operation of these gifts.

This is not to say that leaders should never allow tongues in a large meeting. But the leaders of a large meeting should be in control and have a plan. This could even include planning for how to handle the unplanned or unexpected. For example, the leaders may wish to allow tongues and interpretation from the front area where they control the microphone. Alternatively, a leader—under the unction of the Holy Spirit—may offer an open invitation for someone to share a tongue.

What does not go well is a spontaneous tongue spoken forth from a potentially unknown person during a moment of silence as often happens at the end of a worship song. In such instances, I fully support leaders who take a moment to judge the situation, and then choose to state matter-of-factly, "That was not from God."

BEGINNING TO PURSUE INTERPRETATION

Years back, I was at a home meeting that included several families who had school-age children. One of the leaders—a man I deeply respect—assembled a teaching on the topic of tongues for the children. Toward the end of his teaching he demonstrated his own tongue by uttering about five distinct words in the unknown tongue. When finished, he asked the children if anyone had any questions. A ten-year-old girl raised her hand eagerly and asked, "What does that mean?"

Before I reveal the answer the leader gave, let's consider the possible answers one who utters a tongue publicly as part of a teaching might give if asked the same question. The list below is meant to be representative rather than exhaustive.

a. Good question. That is my regular tongue. It means …

b. Good question. Technically I should have given the interpretation after uttering my tongue before a group of others. It means …

c. Good question. As mentioned before when someone speaks a tongue publicly, as I just did, he should pray for an interpretation. Allow me to pray and give you the interpretation.

d. Those words were praising God, though I do not have a deeper interpretation.

e. I've been speaking this same tongue for a while now. I have been seeking the interpretation through prayer as well as soliciting help from others known to interpret. But so far, I do not have an interpretation other than to tell you I am praising God with those words.

f. I have no idea.

What would your answer be if asked the same question? What do you think would be the most common answer given by someone who has been speaking in tongues—perhaps the same simple tongue—for many years? What would you want your answer to be, if different from your actual answer?

In this anecdotal story from years ago, the teacher in question replied to the ten-year-old girl by saying, "I have no idea." His answer put me into a spiritual tailspin, if such a thing could exist. First, I did not think it was appropriate to utter a tongue out loud before a group (as opposed to under one's breath during prayer) without having an interpretation, or at least planning for one.

However, I realized this leader had merely been demonstrating to the children. If he had been proclaiming praise or thanksgiving on behalf of the group, an interpretation would have been particularly merited. But more importantly, I had been praying in tongues for roughly twenty years by the time I attended that home meeting. And, like this leader, I had no idea what any of the words coming out of my mouth meant.

Thus began my journey into interpreting my own tongue. In my case—and I expect I was not alone—I found interpreting my own tongue somehow more intimidating than interpreting the tongue of another. While I had a complex rather than a simple tongue, there were still many distinct words that appeared with regularity. Those would necessarily have the same meaning from one time until the next.

Or at least so I believed at the time. My actual experience was that not long after interpreting a specific word, it would disappear from my utterances after only a brief window of time (sometimes as little as a few weeks). At the time of this writing, I do not know if others have had or will have the same experience. Additionally, I do not know the reason for the eventual loss of an interpreted word in my utterances. My educated guess is that the Lord wants us to pray for interpretation regularly. We may want the old wine, but He is the Lord who gives us new wine.

The eventual loss of a word not long after gaining the interpretation shouldn't discourage anyone from interpreting their own tongue. I would still advocate praying for an interpretation of your regular tongue because of the richness you can enjoy from understanding words that you regularly utter in your tongue.

I promise it is always worth the effort.

My Conviction Regarding Leadership

A little over a decade ago, I took over the leadership of a mid-week home group and began hosting the group in our home. The group was part of our church community at that time. It included many new believers whose faith was tender and fragile. I empathized deeply with Paul's descriptive words, "babes in Christ" (1 Corinthians 3:1 NKJV). We ate together and sang together during these meetings.

My wife and I also brought a short teaching each week. We were often amazed that the weekly lesson topics which came to our hearts continuously proved to be a preamble to the upcoming Sunday morning sermon. One new believer always had lots of questions for us regarding the teachings—something again that would not be practical in a large Sunday morning meeting, but which worked very naturally among such a small group in our home. We ended each meeting with communion and prayer.

Eventually I developed the conviction to teach on the gifts of the Spirit, including the gift of tongues. The topic of the gifts of the Spirit—especially tongues and prophecy—were both exciting and frightening to these new believers. They did not want to offend with a false prophecy, nor utter a tongue without an interpretation. Who could blame them? We had read out loud the very Scriptures cited in this work!

As the leader of the group, I felt a deep sense of responsibility. And in my prayers to the Lord, I shared this burden. While sharing the burden for only a few days, the solution became obvious to me. I earnestly sought the Lord to grant me the gift of interpretation. I asked that I would be able to interpret any tongue uttered by another in my presence, if they could not interpret it themselves. I also asked that I could interpret any tongue of my own that I would utter before a group.

I continued in this prayer over several days. When I prayed privately in tongues, I believed I was likewise putting this request before the Lord. Two days prior to our next scheduled meeting, I felt a clear sense that my request had been granted, and I received clear instruction from the Lord regarding how to proceed.

I felt a great weight come off of me. In the meetings that followed, members of the group, including some of the new believers, developed the courage to speak in tongues during our meeting. We followed "the rules" and limited the tongues to two or three per meeting. The members also prayed for interpretation. Sometimes they had a very general interpretation such as "I felt I was able to fully express how thankful I feel toward God." But in most cases, I gave the interpretation.

Upon becoming a leader, I felt a conviction to develop the ability to interpret tongues so that we did not need to forbid their utterance or risk having no interpretation. While my position on the subject appears to put me in the minority, I believe anyone entering any kind of group leadership should ask the Lord to give him or her the ability to interpret any tongue spoken in his or her meeting, anytime the speaker is not able to interpret.

My Process for Interpreting Another's Tongue

As I share my process of interpreting another's tongue here, let it be clear to any reader that this process was given to me by God as an answer to my prayer; I know of no detailed instruction given in Scripture on how to interpret a tongue. My process may work for you, or the Lord may give you a different process. He could also tell you simply to "just do it" as I have heard others state anecdotally.

When I interpret, I begin by concentrating deeply on the voice of the person speaking in tongues, every syllable and even the accent in the person's words. I listen carefully to hear if the same word is spoken more than once in the tongue. At the same time, I concentrate inward to hear what words appear in my own mind, seemingly as a reflex to what is being spoken in the unknown tongue.

Aware that the grammatical syntax of the unknown tongue may not put words in the same order as they appear in English, I assemble an interpretation. As I speak forth the interpretation, I may get more insight into the depth of meaning. I may include the deeper meaning in the public interpretation, or share it later with the individual in private. Other times, I may keep it to myself as a gift from the Lord to me as the interpreter—because often delivering the amount of depth given to me would be difficult or take too long to explain in the context of a group setting.

My Process for Interpreting My Public Tongue

When praying in a group, I occasionally feel the unction to pray in the form of a tongue followed by an interpretation. The same could go for worship, but I have personally never felt the unction to sing in a tongue during worship. And given the quality of my singing voice, I don't think I would ever want to sing an interpretation. But that is just me.

Once I begin uttering my tongue, I pay attention to the sounds coming forth as I do with another's tongue. Generally, I have a vague rather than a specific interpretation while speaking. At some point, it seems right to either pause for an interim interpretation, or stop for the full interpretation. As I then interpret, the vagueness is replaced with clarity, very rich meaning, and a sense of how to express that rich meaning in English.

If one wonders, "What is the point? Why not simply pray what you prayed in the interpretation?" I can only say that without speaking the tongue, I would not have been able to articulate what was in my heart and the shared hearts of those in the meeting. A number of times, people have come up to me afterwards to tell me how blessed they were to hear my tongue, and to pray along with the interpretation. Those blessings would have been lost without the steps of first speaking the tongue, and then exercising the gift to interpret it.

Tongues and interpretation are a mysterious and wonderful gift-pair, which I have come to believe is underappreciated, under experienced, and poorly understood. I believe there is an opportunity for the coming generation of believers to enjoy a richer experience of prayer and worship by incorporating tongues and interpretation more effectively.

I should note that the interpretation is never inconsistent with what has been going on during the meeting. If anything, the interpreted tongue adds color, depth, or a sense of completion to what was prayed by others. The ones who express to me their appreciation often explain that what I spoke was exactly what was on their hearts to pray themselves, but somehow richer.

Duty and Responsibility
in Interpreting

There was one instance years back when I interpreted that I wish I could have a chance to do over. I now deeply regret not providing more detail, at least privately to the speaker. During a large group meeting, one of the young leaders spoke up and shared his conviction that we should trust God to speak in tongues publicly and for there to be an interpretation. He was outwardly nervous but determined to step forward in faith. He told the group he would speak a tongue and invited the group to attempt to interpret. I was confident I would be able to interpret, but wanted to allow the speaker or another to utter the interpretation first.

When the young leader spoke out his tongue, it was a simple tongue. I only heard two distinct syllables. The interpretation came to me almost immediately. After ten seconds of silence, I spoke up: "Oh. That was easy."

I now regret saying something so smug. It undoubtedly came across as though I was claiming that this interpretation was a simple or easy thing for me to do, when no one else in the room could do it. Developing a gift of interpretation is not an easy thing to do, and I am not making light of it.

The interpretation was as follows.

> *I need Your love. I need Your love. I need Your deep, deep love. I need Your love. I need Your love. I need Your love.*

The young leader was both pleased to have an interpretation, but also a little disappointed to hear so little. Yet he also appeared to realize he had spoken just two distinct syllables, and accepted that such a simple prayer in tongues might only have a simple interpretation. The truth was there had been much more to the interpretation that I did not share, either with the group that day, nor privately with the young leader afterward.

What else was there? Within the two words the young leader spoke was the depth of this young leader's need, the uniqueness of the Lord's love for this young leader, and just how deep that love was. The tongue described a very deep, intimate, and personal love the Lord felt for the young leader, as well as the sense of relief, satisfaction, and joy the Lord's love gave to him.

INTERPRETING YOUR OWN
TONGUE PRIVATELY

Before providing any guidance from my own experience, guidance from Scripture is in order: Ask. This goes for any gift. Ask and then keep asking until you receive.

In my case, I began interpreting the tongues of others after asking for quite some time and then eventually getting a clear internal sense that my request had been granted. I began interpreting my own tongue after first asking God for the interpretation, and second attempting to interpret using the same process I had used to interpret the tongues of others.

Admittedly, I found it difficult to simultaneously utter my tongue and listen to what I was speaking with the same level of concentration I applied when seeking to interpret the tongues of others. I had to stop and then start over again. I would get out just a few words and then stop and let the sounds sink into my mind. What I found in my case was that the opening words of my tongue tended to be the same set of words. And so even though my tongue was complex, the first words of my utterance were simple. And it was this simple tongue of my own that I sought to interpret first.

Unlike a public interpretation of either my own tongue or the tongue of another, my interpretation of my own tongue when praying privately did not come right away. It was several weeks in fact. But as I continued to listen to my tongue—and to listen for the small voice in my mind interpreting—I became intimately familiar with each word and the subtleties of the accent with which I uttered them.

The accent was not dramatically different from my native North American English. But there were subtle differences. One word I utter currently has a consonant that falls somewhere between how the letter L and the letter D sound in North American English, for example.

When interpreting my regular, personal tongue, key words begin to emerge. These include words that express the Lord's greatness, His love, and what He has done for us. But in my experience, the most meaningful and exciting words to interpret are the words that address God.

WORDS TO ADDRESS GOD MORE INTIMATELY

J esus set off a theological bombshell when He claimed that God was His personal Father.

 "Therefore the Jews sought all the more to kill Him, because He not only broke the Sabbath, but also said that God was His Father, making Himself equal with God."

– JOHN 5:18 (NKJV)

Judging by their reaction, there was no name or title for God that the Jews of Jesus' time understood to mean a *personal* father prior to these statements of Jesus. But He didn't stop when describing God as His own Father. When His disciples asked, "Teach us to pray," Jesus began that prayer with, "Our Father." If an *individual* had asked Jesus, "Teach me to pray,"

I expect Jesus would have opened that prayer with something like, My Father, Father, or even Abba Father.

Scripture teaches that generally when a person speaks or prays in tongues, he or she is speaking to God using a language God gave to that person.

"For he who speaks in a tongue does not speak to men but to God."

– 1 CORINTHIANS 14:2A (NKJV)

It is possible that an interpretation of somebody's tongue—especially a simple tongue—might not address God by name or title. A good friend of mine, for example, has interpreted his regular tongue as, "Sanctify me" with no direct address to God. However, I believe that in most if not all cases, your tongue either directly or indirectly addresses God in some way that includes a name, title, or at least some way in which the person in question is relating to God at the time. Even my friend mentioned above is still relating to Him as one who sanctifies.

As mentioned earlier, the majority who speak in tongues speak with a very limited vocabulary—sometimes even just a single word. My observation is that for those who speak in tongues with a wider vocabulary, including myself, certain words will still appear with regularity.

Think of your own prayers in your earthly language. You probably use one word or combination of words—*God, Jesus, Dear Jesus, Father, Holy Father, Holy Spirit*, or even *Help me God* or *I need You God*—far more often than the sum of your next ten most commonly used words or word combinations.

Additionally, that word or word combination will usually—but not always—be the first thing to come forth each time you pray.

In the previous section, I provided a simple process that has worked for me to interpret my own tongue. Once you have successfully interpreted a single word or word combination in your own tongue, that will lay the foundation for developing the ability to interpret your entire tongue, and then eventually moving on to interpreting the tongues of others.

If you will allow me, please take a moment and perform this simple exercise. Speak the name 'Jesus' out loud. Observe in your mind how much the English word Jesus means to you. The actual word means "God is Salvation." But I expect the name Jesus means much more to you. It probably includes what you know of Jesus' earthly ministry, what He has done in your life and in the lives of your loved ones, and what Jesus promises He will do in the future.

Now take the exercise further and say the words you use most commonly to address God. For example, I personally say "Lord Jesus" when addressing Jesus and "Mighty Father" when addressing God the Father. These addresses I use tie specific qualities of God that I choose to emphasize—and which are 100% consistent with what is taught in Scripture, of course— during my prayer.

I want to highlight how much of a treat it will be to interpret. As you begin to interpret a word, or word combination, it will probably not be a simple one-to-one translation to a similar word in English (or your specific earthly language, if different from English). Instead the word will be rich in depth of meaning. The name or title for God that He has given to you in the private and personal language you share with Him will include the richness of your relationship with Him. And as you come to interpret this word, you will be able to experience that relationship at a deeper level. Think of the pet names parents give to children or the pet names children give to their parents, and then extend that concept to your relationship with God.

As an earthly example, there was a special name I gave to my daughter just before she could talk. Whenever she was particularly happy or joyful, she would let out a sound that in Anglophone might be written, "Deedle-deedle!" I began to call her Deedles.

What did Deedles mean? It was not simply another name for my daughter. Instead, that name captured the joy and happiness she so often expressed at that time in her life. It communicated the joy and closeness I felt toward her whenever she expressed such happiness, as well as encompassing the father-daughter relationship she and I enjoyed at that time.

If you seek Him in this manner, I do not believe the Lord will remain nameless or merely generic in your tongue. Instead, I believe you will discover a new and deeper way to address God, perhaps even a name for God hidden to all others except you. Or you could think of it simply as a word, which once interpreted by you, will express your relationship with God at that time in a way your earthly language could not fully express.

I say *at that time* because in my experience, the name (within my tongue that can be interpreted as my private name for God) changes with some frequency. In order to keep up, I need to interpret my own daily tongue with some regularity. The vocabulary I use—possibly the entire language I use—and especially the most intimate name I use, changes over time.

While writing this book, I repeated the process of interpreting my own tongue, and specifically interpreting how

I was addressing God in my tongue. A simple interpretation of that name could be *The God of the Baptism in the Holy Spirit.* In speaking and interpreting this word, I can feel all three persons in the Trinity. I can also feel that they find so much joy baptizing believers, not with water, but with the very person of the Holy Spirit.

I also feel how God felt toward me when I first received the gift of tongues many years back. And as I pray in tongues today and hear this name for God, I feel His eager anticipation for believers to experience the gifts of tongues and interpretation with anticipation, joy, and wonder. This way of addressing God—unique to me in my prayer language—urges me with conviction to pass on to other believers all that is available in this gift.

FINAL THOUGHTS

While writing this work on interpretation, God used two events to drive home an important lesson to me that I would like to pass on to readers. Interpretation, like all gifts of the Spirit is a gift, not a power.

The first instance was briefly mentioned by Kathleen in her section, but I will share a little more detail here. I was in a rideshare and another rider was speaking in a language I did not recognize. She was not speaking on her phone. I quickly realized that she was speaking in tongues. While I did not believe it was proper to speak in tongues without interpretation in front of others one does not know, I also did not want to interrupt my co-rider's intimate interaction with the Lord in order to admonish her.

Instead, I decided to use the opportunity to practice the gift of interpretation. But the moment I began my attempt to interpret, it was as if a door slammed shut in my mind. I was very surprised. Inside my mind, I asked the Lord what was going on.

The answer I sensed was that the lady in the car was speaking privately to the Lord. Further, she believed that by exercising the gift of tongues, she was keeping what she was saying private from the others present. So, the interpretation of these particular utterances were none of my business. So the Holy Spirit was intentionally withholding the interpretation.

In the second instance, I was in a meeting co-sponsored by multiple church institutions in my home city. Jens, one of the young leaders I mentioned earlier, is known for a powerful gift of tongues and interpretation. During the meeting, he began to utter a tongue. Again, I decided to practice my gift of interpretation. Despite a long and complex tongue, all that came to me was a short verse from Scripture.

When Jens finished his tongue, he then gave a lengthy interpretation. It was roughly the length of his tongue and certainly longer than the single verse that came into my mind when I attempted to interpret. But the interpreted words from this young leader were consistent with the theme of the verse I had received when I attempted to interpret. The interpretation was also consistent with what Jens had been speaking prior to uttering his tongue.

Later, I sought the Lord about the reason for my very limited interpretation. The answer I received was that, in this situation, Jens had the primary responsibility to interpret his own tongue. And as he was fulfilling this responsibility, the only value I could add using the gift was to provide validation of his interpretation, in case there was any challenge to his interpretation in my mind or anyone else's.

The twin gifts of tongues and interpretation are meant to build up the believer in private. They are also meant to build up everyone present when shared in a group setting. As mentioned above, they are gifts, not powers. I believe these gifts, particularly interpretation, are underutilized at present. It is my sincere hope that this book will play a part in awakening a desire across the Body of Christ to experience the full spectrum of what God has for His children in these last days.

CHRIS'S STORY

CHRIS'S STORY

by Chris McKinney

I connected and identified with many aspects of Kathleen and Matthew's teachings and testimonies, and experienced much revelation, learning, and growth along the way—so much so that I felt I had to share at least some of it with readers.

First, one of the connections. Kathleen explores the fact that tongue speakers are, in a sense, on autopilot. I can testify to the reality of this. Whenever I'm praying in tongues, I can actually have detailed, uninterrupted thought processes going on at the same time. For instance, I could be thinking about God, picturing Him on His throne with the angels all around. I could be thinking through a personal issue or an issue involving work. Or, I could just be having the sort of random thought processes many of us experience throughout the day. For example, I could be thinking through what dinner and the evening with my family is going to be like.

But scientists have found through multiple studies that "Multitasking is Scientifically Impossible."[8] MRI scans of the brain reportedly prove that what humans actually do when they think they are multitasking, is to rapidly switch back and forth between one task and another. The result is they don't perform either task as well as they could by focusing on just one thing at a time. I've noticed such rapid "switching" back and forth in my own experiences, for example when I try to listen to two people speaking at one time, or to say, drive a car while also performing another task inside the car.

With praying in tongues, a prayer is coming out of me, sometimes very passionately and intensely, without me ever mentally focusing on the words coming out of my mouth. Of course in this case, it's the work of the Holy Spirit leading my spirit man to pray or speak, but if I had to describe how it feels in the natural, I would say it feels like something my brain must be doing "on autopilot." There's no feeling of switching back and forth, and no interruptions. For the most part, there's just a continuous flow of words coming out no matter what my conscious mind is thinking about.

One difference worth noting between my experience and Kathleen's is that my emotions do get strongly triggered many times while I'm praying in tongues. I may or may not have well-formed conscious thoughts going on when this happens. When I don't have any conscious thoughts going on (beyond maybe trying to picture God's throne in Heaven), and my emotions get strongly triggered, I always feel like my spirit has been touched by the Holy Spirit in some way. I believe that touch from Him triggers these strong emotions, such as overwhelming joy, peace, or just a sense of God's goodness.

Other times it is simply a feeling of closeness and intimacy with Him.

It could also be the subject matter my spirit man is praying about that has caused me to well up with emotion. Perhaps most interesting and compelling is the fact that when I spend a significant amount of time praying in tongues (say 20 minutes or more), I can often walk away from that experience with a strong sense that my faith and trust in the Lord has been boosted tremendously, even though I don't necessarily have a sense of what I prayed about. Others have described to me feeling a strong sense of peace after praying in tongues. There is no right or wrong response to praying in tongues. I think different people have different experiences.

Kathleen also talks about tongues sometimes "not sounding like anything" and I can relate. I had experienced a similar reaction when I first began exercising the gift. What was coming out of my mouth didn't strike me as sounding very much like a "real language" when I first began speaking in tongues. It wasn't just a single phrase over and over, but there was some amount of repetition. However, the biggest issue I had was that I didn't feel like the syllables flowing out of me sounded like real words.

At the same time I was pondering this issue, someone sent me a video of missionaries working in the Philippines. While watching it, I realized that the language spoken by the Filipinos didn't sound like anything to me either. It just sounded like random, broken syllables—a lot like repetitive gibberish.

I suspect that is the case for many languages that aren't Latin-based,[9] or at the very least Indo-European. Hebrew and Arabic are two major exceptions for me personally. Even though they aren't Latin-based, those two languages sound more like real words to me than they do gibberish, even though they are very different from my language.

Latin-based languages sound like real words to us native English speakers because they are so similar to our own. As I was writing this section, I watched a video of someone speaking Swahili. It sounded like broken syllables. Gibberish. Nonsense. If I heard someone praying in Swahili during church, and I didn't know this person spoke Swahili, I would certainly conclude that the person was praying in tongues. And I might even wonder if they had only recently started praying in tongues, such that they weren't very developed in using their prayer language yet.

Kathleen explored whether the devotional, private prayer language tends to be more simple and the special tongues often interpreted for edifying the church tend to be more complex. I found her thoughts on this to be fascinating and as valid as any other potential explanation. However, I do wonder if there is a more simple explanation altogether. Some languages sound like "real words" to a native English speaker, whereas others sound more like gibberish.

It could be that the real answer is a combination of both. Like Kathleen says, *"Speaking in tongues involves speaking mysteries. I don't believe a complete and provable understanding of it is available in this world"*

Agreed.

Some Things I Learned About Interpretation

When I first started out on the journey of interpretation, I was expecting to get some kind of direction or guidance from God. I didn't sit and consciously think through the possibilities, but I believe that internally, I was kind of expecting to get answers to questions in my life—maybe even detailed plans or guidance for situations in my life, and so on.

Instead, what almost always came was praise, thanksgiving, and the continuous expression of a desire to be closer to God. I have pages and pages of interpretation I wrote out during the first month or so, and while there are unique nuances throughout, it's a lot of the same type of stuff. The phrases change, but the subject matter stays fairly consistent. Apparently my spirit man cannot stop telling God how wonderful He is, how beautiful He is, how enamored I am with Him, how much I need Him, and how I want to be closer to Him.

About a month into it, I finally realized that this was actually in line with Scripture:

"Otherwise when you are praising God in the Spirit, how can someone else, who is now put in the position of an inquirer, say 'Amen' to your thanksgiving, since they do not know what you are saying? You are giving thanks well enough, but no one else is edified."

– 1 CORINTHIANS 14:16-17 (NIV)

Paul implicitly notes in this passage two important purposes of praying in tongues: praise and thanksgiving. We also know from verse four of the same chapter that the person who speaks in tongues "builds up" or "edifies" himself or herself. We might conclude, though, from the passage above that the edification is simply a byproduct of praising and thanking God in the Spirit.

If all you ever do with your gift is praise and thank God in a special and unique way, it's well worth the effort.

Be blessed as you move forward into your time of exploration!

A Few Notes About My Process

Again, I asked for and received the gift of interpretation right before I started reading Matthew's section on interpretation, so I didn't really have any instructions to go by. What I do currently is the same thing I did that first day. I speak in my tongue, and then pause after a reasonable amount of speaking and ask for the interpretation.

The Holy Spirit normally gives me one or two words at a time. As soon as I write them down, He gives me more. Sometimes He will give me the rest of a sentence. Other times, I seem to get even a whole sentence or two forming in my mind, but then I have to go back and write each word. When I do that, it's like the idea or concept that had formed in my mind was on point. It normally stays the same. But, the specific wording might develop a little further.

I wouldn't have known this was "normal" if it hadn't been for Matthew's descriptions and guidance. Since I read Matthew's descriptions shortly after receiving an interpretation, they gave me a strong sense of confirmation. One difference for my process is that I don't focus heavily on the actual tongue the way Matthew does. I might notice certain repetitions and such, but in my case, the interpretation just comes to me after I speak the tongue.

I *do focus on hearing* the interpretation though. One of the best examples of this is that sometimes I will oscillate between two words. Then I'll realize that this word I prayed must have a meaning that's a bit unique, without a perfect match in English. Also, sometimes I'll start with a single word in my mind, and if it doesn't quite feel fully developed, I'll chew on it some more. Sometimes it will end up becoming a phrase that means something very similar to the original English word that popped into my mind, but just with more depth of meaning, or more "color" as some might say.

Before I experienced this process and got confirmation from Matthew's descriptions, I would probably have assumed that the interpretation was supposed to come to me chiseled in stone. I might have even assumed that it would completely overpower my ability to think and be part of the process. But as with all other spiritual gifts, we are partners with the Holy Spirit. We have a part to play.

Don't get me wrong, though. The words do come to me. What's fascinating to me about it is that my mind feels blank except for the words of the interpretation. I don't have any deep, distracting, racing, or jumbled thoughts going on during the process. After I ask for an interpretation, my mind is very quiet, which is rare for me.

Another way to say it is that my mind is a blank canvas, and the Holy Spirit is painting. But I (or maybe my spirit man) am the brush, and so my unique characteristics factor into and help form the details of what ends up on the canvas.

Through this process, the interpretation ends up being something I can personally understand and relate to. Each time I write one out, I always read it back silently, and then I pray it back to God out loud. Every time I do that part, this Scripture seems to flash in my mind as I'm about to start:

 "So what shall I do? I will pray with my spirit, but I will also pray with my understanding."

– 1 CORINTHIANS 14:15A (NIV)

SOME INTERESTING EXAMPLES

Again, the vast majority of the interpretations God gave me over that first month were praise, thanksgiving, and strong acknowledgements of my need and desire for Him.

But some of them also contained what I would call personal revelation, mostly about my walk with Him. Here are some portions from my second day of interpretation, after I felt the Holy Spirit nudge me to "keep going":

> *"I always want to be more like You because I know You are good. But, I get hung up on being too good in my own strength. I need to relax and just be with You. That will unlock more power in my life..."*

> *"...I feel like I must be scared of too much intimacy with You, like it's going to change my*

*life too much. But it's actually a good thing.
I need to take more time with You. I always
want more of You but I'm afraid—afraid of
getting too close. I'm afraid of being more like
You because I don't know what I will be like
or how it will change my life. I need to let go
of that fear. I need to just be with You. You
are love! You fill my heart with Your love and
make me like You. Please come in and fill me.
Fill my life with Your love."*

Regarding my third interpretation, I prayed in my tongue
right before sending a brief message of encouragement out to
an email subscriber list. The message I was about to send had
a particular Bible verse and theme, and it was something that
had just popped into my mind. I thought, well, maybe I can
pray in my tongue and the Lord will give me a new message—
one that comes directly from Him—for me to share with these
believers. Here is how the interpretation came out:

*"I always do my best to love others, but I'm not
perfect. So I love them the best I can. I always
want to be the best I can be, and that's a good
thing. But I need more of Your power in my life.
I need You to move and breathe and give life to
everything I do. Please give life to this message."*

So instead of getting a new message, my prayer in tongues
was for God to "give life" to the one I'd already written. I
thought that was interesting. It helped me to relax a little about
my work. Instead of feeling like I have to receive some kind of
specific revelation every time I do something to help others, I

can just share God's truth, encouragement, and love, and ask Him to bless it, anoint it, or "give life" to it.

For my fourth interpretation, I was in a situation where I wasn't quite sure what to do. Another believer had prayed for me and felt like they got direction for me to write an email to a specific person who happens to be a high profile ministry leader. It didn't make any sense to me, but I didn't want to miss anything God might have had for me. So, I wrote an extremely basic email explaining the situation to this ministry leader. Then I prayed in tongues, hoping I would get more insight into exactly what I needed to say in the email, so that I could revise it. Here's what I got:

> *"I don't always know what I'm doing or why but it's okay because I love You and need You to help me. You always help me accomplish what You want me to accomplish even if it doesn't make sense to me. It's okay that it doesn't make sense to me. You know what You are doing and it's always good—the things You are doing— they're always good because You are good. You always know exactly what You are doing even if I don't. You are good. I can trust You. You are special to me. You have a special place in my life. You are good. I need You. Everyday. I need You. You are good. I need You. I need You."*

I felt like this interpretation was the Holy Spirit's way of reminding me that I don't have to worry so much about "getting it wrong" when it comes to His individual direction for my life. He's working through all of various things happening in my life, even if I don't understand what He's doing. This reminder was very good for me, because otherwise I'll sit there and wonder whether I just drastically changed my life by writing (or not writing) an email. Worse yet, I have a tendency to take things further, like wondering if I drastically altered the course of my life by what I said (or didn't say) in the email. As I reflect on all of this, I feel like the Lord must be constantly looking at me and going, "R....E....L....A....X."

Maybe some of you out there can relate.

Another quick note on this one. At this point, I'm not sure if I had read Matthew's examples of the simplistic and repetitive interpretations of tongues. All I remember is that when I did see his descriptions, I received a strong sense of confirmation because I had gotten at least a couple of examples like the ending above that were very simplistic and repetitive.

For my fifth interpretation, I don't recall or have any notes about what was happening that day. I don't recall what might have been on my conscious mind. But it's pretty obvious what my spirit man was thinking about that day:

> "I always love my wife but I need Your help to be the man I'm supposed to be. She's a very good wife, and she loves me very much, and she loves You. She's sweet and kind, and I thank You, Lord, for my wife."

Now, the sixth interpretation I got was perhaps the most profound and important one up to that time. The day before, I had briefly noted the subject matter of Matthew's section called "Words to Address God More Intimately." I really struggled with the concept, because I realized that to be able to address God in an unknown tongue, that meant I would have to call God by an unknown word, or name.

I know from reading the Bible that God's name is incredibly important to Him, and that Jesus is the name above all names.

Yes, He has many names and titles, but I was feeling strongly like we should be sticking to the ones in Scripture. The devil doesn't care what his followers call him. God definitely cares.

So again, I had wrestled with that the previous day. I know I had prayed about it along the way, and asked God to help all of us and give us wisdom and understanding on that topic. I got up that morning, read my Bible, and then said, "Lord, I yield my tongue to You, and I ask You for the interpretation." Here is what I got (I paused at the end of each paragraph and wrote down the interpretation before praying again in my tongue):

> *"I need You more than I know. I love You and want to be close to You and be friends with You. You are my God, but you're also my Friend, my Provider, and my Protector. Bless me today in all the work I'm doing to bring You glory and bless (praise?) Your name. I need You and I love You.*

> *I love You and I need You. You are special to me. You have a special place in my life. You are good. You are amazing. You are wonderful, and I love You.*

> *Jesus, You are my God, but You're also my friend. I need You in my life. I long for Your presence and power in my life. You are amazing to me, Jesus. You are my best friend.*

> *Jesus, You're my best friend. You are so good to me. Thank You for loving me and rescuing me from the devil. Thank you for completing*

Your work on the cross so that we can live in Heaven with You forever. Worthy is the Lamb who was slain. You are worthy, Lord, my God, my Provider, my Savior! In Jesus' name I pray, Amen."

Before that, I had only been referring to God as "You" in my interpretations. Or so I thought. When I went back through everything later on, I noticed in the very first one that I prayed, in the very first sentence, "Bring people together by the power of Your Holy Spirit." I didn't think anything of that at the time. I obviously didn't think of it as being something to analyze or ponder.

But I certainly had not spoken the English words "Holy Spirit" during that prayer. I also had not spoken anything like any of the English names or titles of God which appear in the prayer above. I didn't say anything that sounded like "Jesus," "Yeshua," or any other known name for Jesus. But I had clearly been addressing and referring to Jesus Christ, the One and Only Son of God, during my prayer.

Once I realized that, I also recognized a few other important things. Everything in all of the prayers is 100% biblical. All of the names or titles or characterizations of God in these interpretations are 100% biblical. But going further, I realized it's not just that they're consistent with the Bible. I personally think of them as the same names, titles, and characterizations of God that are found in the Bible, only spoken in a different language.

Names sound different in different languages—if that idea is new to you, you might want to explore the difference between "Jesus" and "Yeshua" or "Yasou" and even "Joshua." You might want to explore the difference between "Jehovah" and "YHWH". Some more earthly examples might be, "Mary, Marie, and Maria" or "John, Johan, and Juan." In fact, if you Google "Alternate forms of the name John" you should find a Wikipedia page which lists over 90 different forms of that one name.[10] Some of them don't look or sound anything like the English version, but somehow it's still the same name.

God's names and titles are what they are. But we can speak them in a different, unique language that the Holy Spirit gives to us. If you think about it, it would be very strange for the Holy Spirit to give us a language, or tongue, that didn't have words for God, His names, titles, character, and nature.

Beyond the interpretations I've already shared, I thought the tenth was interesting because it shows how much our spirits are influenced by God's Word:

> *"Blessed is the one who hears Your Words and obeys. You are upright and steadfast to do what You've promised. I can always count on You. Bless me today I pray, in Jesus' name, Amen."*

I hardly ever use words like "upright" and "steadfast" in my conscious prayers (I tend to say perfect, Holy, and righteous instead), but I know I've read those words many times in certain Bible translations.

Another thing I noticed a couple of months into receiving interpretations is that over and over, I was "blessing" the Lord and saying "Blessed are You, Lord" in many of my prayers. This was a little bit strange to me because I never say that when praying with my understanding. I knew that Scripture contained the phrase "Bless the Lord, O my soul" but I think I had subconsciously chalked that up to a possible translation or language issue, because in my mind, God is the one who blesses.

But, it kept showing up, so I finally decided to Google the concept, and I came across a great explanation (written by John Piper in 1978) of blessing the Lord and calling Him blessed. Piper gives quite a few scriptural examples of this, and explains the concept very well.[11] All of a sudden, it made perfect sense to me to call the Lord blessed and to bless Him. It's just another little nugget of treasure in my spiritual life that came through the gift of interpretation.

Scripture continues to show up in my prayers more and more as I receive interpretations, sometimes with verses pretty close to word for word. For example, here is an excerpt of a recent interpretation:

> *"Bless the Lord, O my soul, and forget not all His benefits. You forgive all my sins and heal all of my diseases... You are always with me and for me, and I will not fear. I will not worry. There is nothing to worry about or fear. You are in complete control. You formed me in my mother's womb, and you've known me since before the world was formed. You foreknew me and predestined me to be conformed to the image of Your Son. Thank You, Jesus, for dying on a cross for me and reconciling me to the Father. Thank You for loving me."*

The 11th interpretation I got was also interesting to me, because it demonstrated to me that my spirit is perfectly connected to God's Spirit, and is therefore thinking about what He's thinking about:

> *"Forever is a long time for people to not know You and to suffer agony and torment. Please*

> *bless me today to reach the lost and fulfill*
> *everything you have for me to do for Your*
> *Kingdom."*

As I write this, I'm a couple of months into receiving interpretations, and doing so has blessed my spiritual life in many ways. For example, God has started giving me interpretations where I was praying for a person I probably never would have thought to pray for with my understanding.

There is one lady at my church that I know, but not very well. I have no idea what might be going on with her. But one day my interpretation read:

> *"Please bless _____ today. She needs a*
> *special blessing today. She is longing for more*
> *spiritually, so I pray for an outpouring of Your*
> *Spirit on her, my sister in Christ."*

Right after that, I had asked for comfort and peace for another lady that I wouldn't normally think to pray for. I wasn't thinking about either of them before praying. The extent of my relationship with both of them is that I say hello when I see them at church.

I have also received personal revelation, answers, and encouragement from the Lord, and it has gone deeper and more specific as I continue to utilize the precious gift I've been given. I believe that as we operate more and more in the spiritual gifts, and in the fullness of those gifts, we have more of God's power to help each other, reach the lost, and build His Kingdom.

*[**Note:** Please bear with me through the rapid-fire style teachings contained in the following sections. It's a lot of information packed into a short space, but I believe this information could be extremely helpful.]*

An Exhortation

I want to leave readers with an important exhortation: As we exercise our spiritual gifts, we should continue to make Bible study a major priority in our lives. Paul tells Timothy in 2 Timothy 1:6:

 "For this reason I remind you to fan into flame the gift of God, which is in you through the laying on of my hands." (NIV)

[**Note:** If you haven't received the baptism of the Holy Spirit, please see the Bonus Material at the end of the book.]

Sometimes our spiritual gifts start only with a small spark or ember. It's up to us to use them, develop them, and cause them to grow into something that will be useful for giving light, protection, warmth, and comfort to ourselves and others.

So, fan your gifts into flame, dear reader. However, please note Paul's other instructions to Timothy:

*"Do not neglect your gift, which was given you through prophecy when the body of elders laid their hands on you. Be diligent in these matters; give yourself wholly to them, so that everyone may see your progress. **Watch your life and doctrine closely. Persevere in them, because if you do, you will save both yourself and your hearers.**"*

– 1 TIMOTHY 4:14-16 (NIV)

Let's take a closer look at what this passage teaches:

- Don't neglect your spiritual gifts.
- Be very diligent about this. Make it a priority to put your gifts into practice and develop them.
- As you operate in the power of the Holy Spirit, you will see a lot of good fruit being produced. Others will see it too. But we still have to be careful to walk out the rest of our Christian life with diligence. Having a fruitful ministry doesn't mean we've "arrived" and can now relax our standards in other areas. Everything needs to be done out of our love for God and others, and we still have to walk in holiness.
- Doctrine is just another word for "teaching." Watch your doctrine, or teaching, closely. Be very careful not to teach or promote false or erroneous teachings.

- Persevering in these matters will lead to "salvation" for yourself and those who listen to you. The Greek word translated "save" is *sozo*, which can mean to rescue, save, heal, or deliver.

Scripture encourages us, as a body, to desire, seek, fan into flame, and practice all of the spiritual gifts. However, there is no substitute for studying, memorizing, meditating on, and immersing ourselves in the Bible. This safeguards us against all kinds of deception. It keeps us free from wrong influences. It keeps us close to the heart of our Father.

I make it a point to always read the Bible right before I pray in tongues and interpret. I want the written words of God recorded in Scripture to be the primary influence in my mind, heart, and life.

GOD STILL SPEAKS

However, as I have continued to operate in this wonderful gift of interpretation, I have gotten what I believe were direct messages from the Lord—the types of messages a body of believers might get by practicing the dual gifts of tongues and interpretation. Here is one such example:

> "You are blessed, Chris—chosen by Me. Why do you worry and fear? There is nothing for you to fear. Believe in Me. Trust in Me. Trust in My goodness and My love for You. Trust in My provision for you. Trust in My sovereign reign, power, and authority. Receive the blessings I have for you. You are cared for. You are provided for. You are in My hands—cradled in My arms. You are Mine. I chose you. Rest in Me."

That interpretation[12] was given to me the very next day after a doctor ordered a biopsy for a lump in my neck. Even though I had gotten through most of the fear about the medical problem at that point, I was now upset that I was going to have to pay $6000 out of pocket for medical expenses. $6000 happened to be the exact amount our publishing company needed to produce and launch this book, so the whole thing was starting to seem like an attack from the enemy—and it felt to me like he was getting the upper hand in some ways.

God took the opportunity to remind me that He is in complete control, and that I don't ever have to worry about provision (By the way, God provided exactly $6000 total cash from two unrelated, both completely unexpected sources just a few weeks after this—right before we started getting medical bills in the mail).

That was the fourth direct message (meaning it came in the form of a message written from God's perspective rather than my own) I received from the Lord through the gift of interpretation. The previous three were similar, but a little more specific to certain situations I was dealing with at the time. When the first such message came to me, I did not ask for or expect anything different than the prayers I had already been getting during my interpretations. It just came to me, and I quickly realized I was writing from God's perspective rather than my own.

One thing I thought about later on is that I've heard many pastors and Bible teachers say over the years something to the effect that, "Prayer is not just talking to God. It's also listening." I've even heard pastors who don't believe the gift of prophecy is active and available for today's believers teach that "prayer is two-way communication." If God is speaking, isn't that divine revelation? Isn't the biblical definition of prophecy simply "a divine revelation?" So my personal view is that we shouldn't consider it strange for God to respond to us during prayer, even (or especially) when that prayer is in a tongue.

TEST EVERYTHING

With those messages from the Lord's perspective, and even with the personal prayers I write down as I'm given the interpretation, one of the first things my mind does is scan to make sure everything is scriptural. Under Old Testament law, the standard for testing prophetic revelation was very strict, and very harsh. Basically, prophets were allowed to speak, but if anything they said in regard to the future did not come to pass, they were considered to be a false prophet. The penalty for a false prophecy was to be stoned to death, just as it was for many other violations of the Mosaic law.

Thank God we live under a much better covenant! According to New Testament instruction, there is now a much different standard that we should use to deal with prophetic revelation. This new standard is outlined for us by Paul in his first letter to the Thessalonians, and can be described as follows.

First, we should never despise any prophetic revelation that comes to us. Despising the gift of prophecy and other prophetic gifts, or treating them with contempt, is a clear and direct violation of Scripture. Second, we should always test every prophetic revelation. Third, we should always hold fast to every prophetic revelation that "is good."

While we can elaborate on how to test, that's basically the entire standard. We never despise prophecy, we test every prophetic revelation which comes to us outside of Scripture, and we hold fast to whatever part(s) of the message or messages which are "good." No stoning is involved. There is no mention of finger-pointing, accusing, blaming, condemning, or arguing among bodies of sincere believers who are seeking the Lord and His gifts.

*"Do not quench the Spirit. Do not despise prophecies, but test **everything**; hold fast what is good."*

– 1 THESSALONIANS 5:19-21 (ESV)

PROPHECY OF SCRIPTURE:
NO TESTING REQUIRED

It should be noted that "prophecy of Scripture" is different from any prophetic revelation we might encounter outside of Scripture. How do we know that? The Bible itself puts "prophecy of Scripture" in a different class than divine revelation which comes to us through any of the spiritual gifts.[13] Peter writes:

*"Above all, you must understand that no **prophecy of Scripture** came about by the prophet's own interpretation of things."*

– 2 PETER 1:20 (NIV)

Paul also clearly teaches that all Scripture is inspired by God (2 Timothy 3:16). The divine revelation contained in Scripture does not need to be tested. You could test Scripture's veracity and accuracy, but it will always pass the test. It is the ultimate standard of truth against which we test everything else. For a biblical example of this principle in action, we can look to Acts Chapter 17. Examining the Scriptures to see how Paul's teachings stacked up against them was how the Bereans determined what was true.

"Now the Berean Jews were of more noble character than those in Thessalonica, for they received the message with great eagerness and examined the Scriptures every day to see if what Paul said was true."

– ACTS 17:11 (NIV)

Prophecy Outside of Scripture Has Always Existed

The Old and New Testaments are both crystal clear on the fact that not all prophecy and divine relevation ended up getting recorded in Scripture, even back when the Bible was still being written. In the Old Testament (in 1 Samuel 10), we read that Saul prophesied, just as Samuel said he would, but we don't have access to the divine revelation God gave him. Maybe it was specific to him personally—we simply don't know.

Another example is when we are told in 1 Kings 18 that Obadiah hid 100 of God's prophets in a cave. We don't know who they were or what they were prophesying. We don't have access to that information in the Bible because obviously those prophecies weren't "prophecy of Scripture." There are other instances, in the Old Testament and the New Testament, of God giving prophetic revelation to His people and then not recording the prophetic revelation in Scripture (see Numbers 11:25 and Acts 21:9 for examples).

There might be people who struggle with the question of why God would give prophetic revelation outside of Scripture. A few obvious reasons have already been discussed in this book, and are confirmed in Scripture. A few such reasons are:

- To alert us to prayer needs that people might have, or situations they might be facing.
- To receive divine guidance that is specific and personal to an individual or a group (e.g., I may have a hard time figuring out which job to take strictly by reading Scripture).
- To develop a closer and more intimate relationship with the Holy Spirit.
- To receive specific, personalized encouragement, exhortation, or comfort from the Lord. For example, God may address specific fears or worries that you have, or that another person has.

There are probably quite a few other good reasons why God may choose to speak or reveal information beyond what is already recorded for us in Scripture.

Other Ways to Test

Another important way such divine revelation can be tested is by sharing it with other members of the body that we're connected with. Other believers can pray about a message or some guidance we feel we have received from the Lord, and let us know what they think. They may have the gifts of discernment, prophecy, words of wisdom, or other relevant gifts that come into play for the testing process.

This type of approach is found in Scripture when Paul is instructing the Corinthians on orderly worship. He basically tells them to take any prophetic messages they receive from gifted members of their congregation, and run those messages by other gifted people in their congregation.

"Two or three prophets should speak, and the others should weigh carefully what is said."

– 1 CORINTHIANS14:29 (NIV)

Another way to test is to just do it! This method will only be appropriate in certain situations. But let's just say for example that you believe God reveals to you a great solution for a challenge you've been wrestling with at work. If the cost of trying the solution isn't onerous, and doesn't mean taking a ton of risk, the right way to test it might be to simply try it out and see whether it carries God's blessing with it.

But even in that instance, you could "test" in a limited way before committing major time and resources to the proposed solution. You're still diligently and wisely obeying the command to test the revelation you believe you have gotten.

Whichever method is most appropriate, the key is to be sure to choose at least one. The testing process is important, but it might be especially easy to forget that when interpreting our own tongue. So we have to make it a point to establish some discipline in this area. The last thing we want to do is make a major life decision and say, "Well, God told me through an interpretation to do XYZ, so I didn't question it."

Remember that God does speak and reveal things through spiritual gifts, but He also tells us to test everything, and then to hold fast what is good. Apart from knowing that instruction, we may be inclined to feel like we're doing something wrong by examining, weighing, and testing prophetic revelation. But it is actually a violation of Scripture *when we fail* to do the examining, weighing, and testing.

PERFECT GOD,
IMPERFECT PEOPLE

I would caution here (and perhaps simultaneously encourage) that as accurate and mind-blowing as prophetic revelation can sometimes be, we are ultimately all doing the best we can in spite of our imperfections and limitations. Even the testing process is not perfect or always perfectly clear, as believers who are being led by the Holy Spirit can still hold different convictions or come to different conclusions (see Acts 20:22, 21:4, and 21:9-14 for a clear example of this principle).

In my understanding, all of the spiritual gifts in the New Covenant age are partnerships between the believer and the Holy Spirit. The individual is not removed from the process, and our "hearers" are not perfect. Besides that, each gift is just one tool in the collective toolbag (or weapon in our arsenal, depending on the context) the Lord has given us. I personally think God designed the New Covenant gifts this way because

He doesn't want us to become too highly focused or overly reliant on a single gift or a single person within the Body.

I know that I don't hear and understand and apply everything perfectly, and I cannot stress that point enough. I am fallible, and I don't know of anyone on the earth today who hears, processes, understands, and applies divine revelation with anything close to perfection. In fact, I generally try to be careful to present revelation with humility, e.g. "I believe the Lord told me…" versus "God said."

There have been two times I can recall in my life when I was not careful to frame something that way, but instead sort of carelessly presented a message as something "God told me." Both times I did that, one of which was recent, I was proven to be wrong, or at least inaccurate.

I think in those cases, most often, I did hear the Lord speaking or revealing things to me, but then I added something to God's message, or applied it in a way that He never intended. But it is also possible to hear a completely different voice—the wrong voice—especially if that voice is telling us something our flesh wants to hear. I don't think God wants us to live in constant fear of this, but He simply wants us to be careful.

So yes, I'm fine with acknowledging that I make mistakes because we all do. All glory goes to God (see Romans 3:4). My goal is not to point people toward myself anyway, but rather to Jesus—the only One any of us should be looking to for answers. I always want to point people to Him, and I thank Him that He doesn't hold any of our mistakes against us.

Of course I try to be as accurate and truthful and as careful as I possibly can, but please don't let your faith depend on me. Instead, trust that God is working in your life right now and speaking to you and giving you everything He wants you to have. That is what He does for me. Since I have been operating in this gift of interpretation, I believe I'm hearing Him a lot more clearly than I ever have. I believe I am closer and more intimate with the Lord than I have ever been. And a lot of the direction, guidance, and revelation I've gotten has been incredibly helpful to me, so there are clear benefits.

WE CAN'T BURY
OUR TALENTS

When you're first starting out with new spiritual gifts, you are bound to make a few mistakes. Let me assure you that it's okay. God is big enough to handle our missteps. Often, the operation of our gifts requires some level of faith. In other words, there is risk involved.

As with any area of life, we don't want to be reckless or careless, but more importantly, we don't want to shrink back in fear. Recall in the parable of the talents that the servant who buried his talent due to fear was called "wicked."

When you feel the prompting of the Holy Spirit to step out and move in a gift, ask for courage and then do it. I normally have some level of regret when I make a mistake even though I was trying to do the right thing. But I usually have *a lot more regret* when I miss an opportunity to minister to and bless someone because I shrank back in fear.

Still, if either of those things happen to you, be encouraged that the Lord is incredibly forgiving, and He wants you to bounce back quickly. He doesn't want you to wallow in regret, or to lose confidence in the gifts He has given you. He works through imperfect people all day, every day.

EXAMPLES
OF HUMILITY

Personally, I believe the imperfect nature of our operation of the spiritual gifts is why we don't see very many believers in the New Testament using the phrase, "Thus says the Lord," even though that phrase was commonly used by the Old Testament prophets. New Testament believers would have studied those prophets extensively, yet for the most part, they don't go around using that phrase when imparting divine revelation.

I want to be clear that we can't say that it's always wrong to use that phrase in the New Covenant age. Some may feel led to use it, and there is instruction from at least one New Testament verse which would back up a person who feels led to present divine revelation that way (1 Peter 4:11). There is also at least one example in the New Testament of someone (who was confirmed as a prophet) using the phrase, "Thus says the Holy Spirit" (see Acts 21:11 ESV).

However, most of the time what we see—even with what ended up being New Testament *prophecy of Scripture*—is that the individual takes a relatively humble posture of simply explaining their belief or position about a topic or situation. Peter acknowledges Paul's letters as being Scripture (2 Peter 3:16) yet Paul himself never states that they are Scripture, or presents them as the Word of God (at least that I am aware of). I have wondered at times if Paul even realized he was writing Scripture. He teaches and instructs with the authority that Jesus gave him, but I don't see any evidence that he was in a routine habit of saying "Thus says the Lord" (or any variant of that phrase).

Sometimes Paul's presentation of information depends on the teaching or revelation being discussed. At times, he explicitly notes that he is only giving his personal preference or convictions (see 1 Corinthians 7:6-7 and 7:25 for examples). But when discussing the truth of the essential teachings of the Gospel, Paul uses very strong, authoritative language (Galatians 1:8). The ultimate point here is that wisdom and discernment should be used in deciding when and how to communicate divine revelation.

THE BLESSINGS OF GOOD
PROPHETIC REVELATION

That brings me back to a crucial point: we have Scripture as the absolute standard of truth for anything that might convey any kind of teaching or theology. Right after I get a message which comes to me as being worded from the Lord's perspective, I immediately test it against my knowledge of Scripture, as I do with all the others.

In the case of the direct message I shared earlier, I didn't find anything unscriptural. Instead, I found that everything in the message was good—it all lines up with Scripture. There was no specific individual direction that required further testing by sharing it with others, and asking for their feedback. Therefore, I decided to hold fast to all of it. It was just basic encouragement to trust in the Lord and His goodness and provision for me, so the testing was fairly easy and straightforward for that one.

While they don't carry the same weight that Scripture carries due to its unquestionable perfection and authority, these messages of personal comfort and encouragement—as well as exhortations from God to trust in Him and keep moving forward in His plans—have been a tremendous help to me when I really needed it most. They helped me overcome worry and fear, and put more trust and confidence in Jesus Christ.

THE HOLY SPIRIT ALWAYS PRODUCES GOOD FRUIT

O perating in this gift has produced a lot of good fruit in my life. There were some interpretations which I read over and over, and they comforted me greatly during a time of need. Maybe these are just a few of the reasons Paul exhorts us, *"Therefore, my brothers and sisters,* **be eager to prophesy, and do not forbid speaking in tongues."** (1 Corinthians 14:39 NIV)

Beyond the fact that these personal revelations from God are full of messages that line up with Scripture, it's worth noting that Scripture itself does show up in these revelations (which are worded from the Lord's perspective) just like it does when I pray in the Spirit (from my own perspective). Here is one such example:

"You are always in my thoughts. I never stop thinking about you. Consider the birds. They do not labor or spin, yet I feed them. Are you not much more valuable than them? You are my chosen servant. You are mine. I am guiding you. I am moving you with My hand. You are on My path..."

That message came to me at a time when I had been wrestling with whether or not I was moving in the right direction in certain areas of my life. I felt assurance and peace that I was on the right path after receiving this message.

Since that time, God has given me very strong confirmation of many of the revelations I am receiving through the tongue-interpretation gift combination. For example, He has given me several advance directives that have proven crucial to me walking out His will during certain times, and even at certain events I attended. Both myself and others have experienced amazing blessings as a result of me faithfully operating in this gift. I consider that to be very good fruit.

SPIRITUAL GIFTS AND SOUND DOCTRINE ARE INSEPARABLE

I hope to share more about those revelations and experiences in a future book, but I want to make the point here that our spiritual gifts should increase the fruit of God's Spirit in our lives and the lives of others. God's people should not be opposed to experiencing His supernatural power, resolving only to read about it instead. God makes it clear over and over in the New Testament that He gives prophetic revelation to His people, and that He will distribute His spiritual gifts exactly as He sees fit.

Obedience to the Holy Spirit is an important part of living a victorious Christian life. So we shouldn't "throw out the baby with the bathwater," so to speak, by closing ourselves off to the spiritual gifts in an attempt to guard ourselves against deception. This is actually a direct violation of Scripture. For example, we can't "be eager to prophesy" and also closed off to the gift of prophecy at the same time. The moment we neglect or deny the spiritual gifts, we are by definition outside of sound Scriptural doctrine.

So, it is certainly possible to be open to the Holy Spirit and to His gifts, while always keeping up a healthy guard against error. In fact, my position is that one can't be fully guarded against error without being completely submitted to the Holy Spirit and the operation of His gifts, simply because Scripture is full of clear commands for us to do those very things.

As passages like 1 Timothy 4:1-3 make clear, there are other types of deception that we must guard against. We should never trade away the clear and authoritative revelation given to us in the Bible by exchanging it for supposed "revelation" that doesn't line up with the Bible. The Holy Spirit will never give us any message or tell us anything that doesn't line up with the clear teachings of the full counsel of the Bible.

Also, if anything we're doing makes studying the Bible seem boring, unfruitful, or less interesting by comparison, I would say that isn't very good fruit being produced. I've actually caught myself slightly drifting in that direction a time or two. It's natural to be really excited about something that is new, so just try to be aware of that risk.

We can mitigate that risk by continuing to study the Bible as we operate in our gifts, and making sure we have a very strong foundation in the Truth. We need to be active in a church full of strong, mature, Spirit-filled, Bible-believing Christians. We must stay connected to other believers, and let them bring accountability, correction, and wisdom into our lives when necessary.

We must guard the faith that God has entrusted to us. The Christian faith, as clearly outlined in the Bible, includes the

Holy Spirit and all of His gifts, so we have to guard those gifts, desire them, seek them, and operate in them. Simultaneously, we must be careful not to let anything or anyone turn us away from our genuine faith in the Lord Jesus Christ, which is more precious than gold.

 "Timothy, guard what has been entrusted to your care. Turn away from godless chatter and the opposing ideas of what is falsely called knowledge, which some have professed and in so doing have departed from the faith."

— 1 TIMOTHY 6:20-21 (NIV)

BONUS MATERIAL

THE BAPTISM OF
THE HOLY SPIRIT

by Chris McKinney

During a prison ministry small group that I co-led in 2016, I received the baptism of the Holy Spirit. I believe that all Christians are spiritually united with the Holy Spirit at the moment of salvation. However, Scripture clearly describes another experience of being immersed, or baptized, in the Holy Spirit. Scripture also describes "being filled with the Spirit." The purpose of the baptism of the Holy Spirit is given by Jesus in Acts 1:8, where He tells the disciples that they will receive power to be His witnesses when the Holy Spirit comes upon them.

Power to be His witnesses is something we should all desire and seek! Unfortunately, I can't give anyone an exact formula for how to be baptized in the Holy Spirit. All I can do is share my own experiences and insight in the hope that it helps those seeking this blessing.

First, I'll give a little background about my history with the Lord. While I used to pray as far back as I can remember, it wasn't until I was 10 years old that God saved me. I walked with the Lord as closely as I could from the ages of 18-20, but then sadly lived as a prodigal from the ages of 20-34.

In 2012, I realized I was in a pig pen, and I went back to my Father's house. By 2016, God had been working in my life for four years to remove various things such as selfish ambition, a struggle with submission to earthly authority, unforgiveness, and fear. Looking back now, I realize He was basically just getting me to a place where I was completely yielded to Him in every area of my life.

In the prison small group, we had been going through Pastor Jimmy Evans' book, *Ten Steps Toward Christ*. As we went through the chapter on the baptism of the Holy Spirit, I recognized that something was missing from my spiritual life. The baptism of the Holy Spirit is as plain as day in Scripture, and I didn't have it, even though I had been walking as closely as I could with the Lord for the previous four years.

So I asked some men—inmates in our small group—who had already received the baptism to lay hands on me and pray for me to receive it. As I was driving home that night, I prayed in tongues—really prayed in tongues—for the very first time. I went into the prison to minister to these guys, and they ended up ministering to me!

So I think there were three keys to me receiving the baptism of the Holy Spirit:

1. A time of preparation in which God got me to a place of complete surrender for the major areas of my life.

2. I asked for Him to come in and fill me.

3. Others who had already been baptized in the Spirit laid their hands on me and prayed for God to fill me and to impart spiritual gifts to me.

Regarding number one, I'll try to explain a little further. Over time, God would put His finger on various areas of my life to show me that I was still holding on to—or being held captive by—things like greed, selfish ambition, my own plans for my life, or fears and reservations that I had. I wasn't fully trusting him in certain areas.

For example, I had a major fear of and resistance to public speaking that had plagued me for as long as I could remember. I realize now that it all could be traced back to an experience I had at four years old. I was asked to get up in front of a crowd and speak a line in a play. Instead of saying my line, I burst into tears, and the crowd erupted with laughter. I had been emotionally scarred by that at a very young age.

Since our society basically forces everyone to do various forms of public speaking in high school, college, career, and so on, I'd had plenty of terrible experiences. Often, so much adrenaline was released into my bloodstream due to the fear, that when it came time for me to speak, I could barely get words to come out of my mouth. It was always incredibly embarrassing, and it always made the others present uncomfortable as well.

God's deliverance and healing for me involved having me stand up in front of the 80+ people in our larger prison ministry group and talk to them. I knew God was telling me to do this, and decided to simply face the fear head on. I was afraid with every step as I walked to the front of the room to take the microphone, but I went anyway. When I got up there and turned around, God's perfect peace came over me, and I began speaking with total comfort and ease. Every time since then that He has called me to do it, my experience is the same. He's right there with me, and I have total peace.

That's just one example. There were several instances like that where I had to face certain things head on and just trust God with them. I had to yield to Him and let Him have His way with me. I realized looking back, that these types of experiences accelerated in the months leading up to me receiving the baptism. God was working to help me be completely yielded to Him, and to trust Him in every area. That doesn't mean I reached some level of perfection, but I think He knocked down the larger barriers of distrust, fear, and self-will that I had going on.

On the second key, I would just note that the Holy Spirit doesn't force Himself on anyone. We need to be open to the Holy Spirit and His gifts. My exhortation to anyone who has grown up being taught that there is no such thing as a "baptism of the Holy Spirit" is to simply open your Bible and see what it says about this topic. Acts 1:5, Mark 1:8, John 1:33, Ephesians 5:18, and Acts 2:4 are good starting points, but there are many other relevant verses and passages.

Next, I would encourage you: Don't worry about what people are going to think of you. You don't want to miss out on one of God's greatest blessings because you're concerned about man's opinions. You can't imagine the joy and the power that will come into your life once you are immersed in God's Spirit! Don't miss it!

Regarding the third key, I would again encourage you to study the Bible. You can find many examples of spiritual gifts being imparted—and the baptism of the Holy Spirit taking place—when believers who have already received those things pray and lay hands on others who have not yet received them. It seems to be the most common method God uses for sure, though I don't believe there is any Scripture which indicates that it's an absolute requirement in every case.

I also want to share a couple of other cases I'm familiar with. I mainly want to share these other cases to show that it doesn't happen the same way for everyone. There is also some helpful insight from these specific experiences.

My wife is the first example I want to share. A day or two after I received the baptism in the Holy Spirit, she wanted it too! I laid my hands on her and prayed for her to be baptized in the Holy Spirit. She began praying in tongues shortly thereafter. Months went by, and she never expressed anything besides a normal acceptance and affinity for her new gift.

Once I can recall asking her if she would like to pray in tongues with me. I can't remember if I had any thoughts about interpretation in my mind. I think I just wanted us to be able to share a new spiritual gift and experience, and I didn't realize there might be anything inappropriate about doing it together. But when we went to try it, she felt very awkward about it, and honestly I did too. It just didn't feel right. I tried to pray in my tongue sitting there with her, and it felt super weird. When I asked her if she wanted to have a go at it, she said no! She said she just didn't feel right about it.

After reading Matthew's explanation on this, I realize now that we were only able to pray a personal prayer language in tongues. We weren't intended to "speak" out in tongues in front of others in order to deliver a message. Besides, neither of us had the gift of interpretation, and again, I don't think we were asking for it either.

A few months down the road, my wife and I went through something called Freedom Conference at my church. It's held twice a year, and many people receive the baptism of the Holy Spirit at that conference. We had already received the baptism as far as we knew, but really that conference is all about getting freedom and healing from the past and anything that is hindering us, so we wanted to be thorough in pursuing God's freedom, deliverance, and healing.

Attending the conference involves going through prayer lines multiple times to receive ministry for different areas of our lives. On one of the occasions, a lady prayed with my wife. The lady began to speak in tongues, and then very intensely she pointed her finger at my wife and said, "Receive the gift of the Holy Spirit and speak in tongues right now!"

At that moment, my wife began to speak in tongues. Later on that day, she told me about the whole experience, and explained that she received the baptism of the Holy Spirit. I said, "No, you've already received it."

She explained, "No, it must not have been real before. This was different. It was almost involuntary. I was overcome by the Holy Spirit, and it was very powerful." So for a long time, we believed that it must not have "been real" for her the first time.

By the way, I should pause and note that praying and speaking in tongues is not the same thing as being baptized in the Holy Spirit. It is just the most common manifestation and sign of being baptized in the Holy Spirit, both in Scripture and in modern experience.

What I now believe is that my wife was baptized in the Holy Spirit the first time around. She was praying in tongues for many months before the conference. I believe that what happened at the conference is that the gift to *speak in tongues publicly* was imparted to her. She can now speak in tongues in a way that goes beyond the personal prayer language God gave her, and someone should be able to interpret what she says when she operates in this gift.

This is a realization which hit me after my older brother's recent experience. His experience was very similar to my wife's. A couple of years ago, while he was on a mission trip with our church, he asked people to pray for him to receive the baptism of the Holy Spirit. During that trip, he did experience an infilling and he prayed in tongues. However, he says he knew even during the experience that what he had received "was only partial." He felt that he had somehow received a partial infilling or baptism of the Holy Spirit, and he longed for the fullness of it.

Thinking that praying in tongues was something that would always sort of come upon him with great power, he did not continue the practice at home. Instead, he continued to ask for the complete baptism of the Holy Spirit, and he would often ask people to lay hands on him and pray for him to receive it. But nothing happened for the next 18 months or so.

Then, in late May of 2019, we all went to a weekend conference at Word Alive International Outreach in Oxford, Alabama. My younger brother and I, and our wives, all went on Friday night. My older brother, his wife, her mother, and my mother all went on Saturday night. We all had amazing experiences there, and I'm sure I'll write more about those one day.

But to stay on topic, I'll just share my older brother's experience here in this book. He went into the conference with great anticipation. In addition to Pastor Kent Mattox and the awesome team at Word Alive, there were some special guests. The flowing oil Bible team was there (see CalledWriters.com/FlowingOil for more info). Pastor Todd Smith, and his baptism team from the North Georgia Revival were there. My brother didn't know a lot about either of these ministries before the week leading up to the conference, and I had not yet heard of the North Georgia Revival myself.

In fact, the way we all ended up at this event is that I had read about the flowing oil Bible in *GODSPEED Magazine*. There was an article that had been written about this amazing miracle and ministry before I came on board with *GODSPEED*. I had followed up reading that article by watching several YouTube videos which contained information about the Bible and the oil, along with interviews of the team.

So I was familiar with the flowing oil Bible and the people involved, but I hadn't thought about their ministry for several months. However, at this time, I was in need of healing for a medical problem I was having, so the thought came to me to look up the flowing oil Bible people. When I looked them up, I found that they were going to be a couple of hours north of us in less than ten days. I decided to go and then invited my family members.

During the day on Saturday, those of us who had gone to the conference on Friday night were excitedly calling and texting about our amazing experiences there, while trying not to give away too many details. So my older brother went into Saturday night's event with great excitement and anticipation—he was really hoping "this would be it." He was hoping this would be what he had prayed for all this time.

After the worship and message, there was a time of prayer and ministry. Water baptisms were happening. People were being healed, delivered, and touched by the Lord. Worship music was still going. Hearts were crying out for more of God's presence and power. And there were long prayer lines. Jerry Pearce, of the flowing oil Bible team, apparently doesn't like for people to have to wait in line all that time to receive God's blessings.

On both nights, Jerry went around through the prayer lines and anointed people, laying the actual flowing oil Bible on their heads. It was visibly clear that God's power and presence and blessing were coming over everyone Jerry touched with his Bible. The fruits of the Spirit such as joy, peace, and self-control were clearly evident in what was happening.

Jerry's wife would also walk around with him at times, praying for people and ministering to people. My brother sat and waited patiently as Jerry made his way around the large auditorium. Finally, he came close to my brother, and my brother began to get really excited, continuously praying and asking God to receive an infilling of the Holy Spirit.

But somehow, amidst the large crowd and the fluid ministry process that was happening, Jerry came close without actually making it to my brother. Then he headed in a different direction altogether. My brother, still praying *silently*, said to the Lord, "No! Lord, please bring him back over here. I'm not going to try to force anything to happen, but I want this. I want You. Please bring him back."

At that moment, seemingly out of nowhere, Jerry, from a different section of the auditorium, looked up at my brother with a piercing gaze, pointed his finger straight at him, and said loudly, "The Lord hears you. I'm coming back over there!"

This story simultaneously gives me chills and brings me to tears each time I hear it or tell it. Jerry indeed made his way back over, and he laid the Bible on my brother's head. My brother felt the power of God run through his entire body, and it caused him to gently sit down as his legs went weak.

He continued to raise his hands in praise to God as he experienced God's power and presence in a unique way. At that moment, Jerry's wife came up behind my brother, again without any request or prompting from any human being, and simply touched the back of my brother's hand with the tip of her finger.

Instantly, my brother began speaking loudly and powerfully in a tongue. He describes what happened as a blissful, joyful, and powerful experience. He says it was involuntary except for the fact that he could have stopped it if he had wanted to. Of course, he didn't want it to stop. This is what he had prayed and longed for over the previous couple of years.

Now, it's certainly possible that he somehow didn't receive the baptism of the Holy Spirit back on that mission trip a couple of years prior. However, I don't believe that's the case at all. And since there is no mention of a partial baptism or a partial infilling in Scripture, I really pondered his experience.

Then one day it hit me out of nowhere. Both my brother and my wife spoke in tongues powerfully and almost involuntarily *in front of other people*. I had not done that even though the people praying over me were asking God for that to happen, and even trying to encourage it. Instead, the gift I received came to me (or manifested) when I was in my car, by myself, on the hour-long drive home from the prison.

And while I had a strong sense that I was not generating the words, I did initiate the experience in some sense by trying to pray in tongues. Once I opened my mouth to start, it came flowing out of me. But *I did start it* by opening my mouth and moving my tongue, and it's been that way for me every time since.

What my brother and my wife describe about speaking out loudly and publicly in a tongue, in my mind, indicates that they have a fuller gift—one which is meant to be spoken in front of others who can interpret.

My personal conclusion is that once received, you don't have to question the baptism of the Holy Spirit, even if there is a longing inside of you for something more powerful. Most likely, the longing you're feeling is for more of God's anointing and power in your life. He's wanting to give you more—a different spiritual gift or gifts, deeper or expanded use of those gifts, more boldness and power to walk in them—and He's putting the desire inside of you to seek Him for those things.

But, since there's nothing in Scripture that says it can't happen, it could also be the case that being baptized with God's Spirit doesn't come all at once for every person. On the other hand, it can definitely come to some people instantaneously at the moment of salvation, as there are several examples of this in Scripture as well as modern day testimony.

It can also come instantaneously to people who have been saved for many years—even if they aren't looking for it—when they physically get in places where the Holy Spirit is moving, such as the North Georgia Revival (or one of the many offshoots now spreading around the country). Sometimes just getting near a great move of God means experiencing His power, deliverance, healing, impartation of His gifts, and so on that we would not receive if we didn't simply decide to go and take part in what He is doing.

Whatever route you decide to take, keep asking Him for the baptism, keep asking Him to fill you, and keep seeking, loving, and pursuing God with all of your heart, mind, soul, and strength. You will undoubtedly end up in a wonderful place!

OUR INVITATION TO YOU

If you have a testimony regarding what the Lord has done in your life through the gift of tongues or through tongues and interpretation, and you believe your testimony would edify others, we invite you to email us.

Tongues.Testimony@gmail.com

Please note that we cannot promise we will be able to reply to all emails.

For more writing by anointed authors, or to connect with us online, please visit:

CalledWriters.com
GodGeekBlog.blogspot.com
Facebook.com/CalledWriters/
Instagram.com/AuthorChrisMcKinney
Facebook.com/MessagesfromGodDevotional
Facebook.com/AuthorChrisMcKinney/

Honoring Craig Davis

Called Writers Christian Publishing author Craig Davis went home to be with the Lord on November 13th, 2019. During the last 17 months of his life, we were honored to be able to work with him to document a legacy that will last for generations.

Craig and his family fought through many intense and painful battles while drawing ever nearer to the Lord. They experienced deep trials and troubles, as well as amazing mountaintop victories. When the cancer returned for a fourth time, Craig wanted to be healed, and he believed God for healing. We believed with him, and now he is completely healed and whole in the arms of his Savior.

But perhaps more than anything else he desired, Craig longed for everyone to know Jesus. He also wanted people everywhere to keep fighting for their miracles, and never give up hope.

Along with his six children and all the many ways he served the Lord, Craig's book, *Never Give Up Hope: Waging War With Cancer* represents a small part of his legacy. His life has already touched the lives of many others, but we hope and believe it will continue to touch many more.

If you are going through anything difficult and painful, we believe Craig's legacy, as documented in his book, would be a major source of inspiration and encouragement for you.

Never Give Up Hope: Waging War With Cancer is available now on Amazon.

MESSAGES FROM GOD:
AN ILLUMINATED DEVOTIONAL

by Kathleen Schwab and Therese Kay

*M*essages from God: An Illuminated Devotional is a full color five-week devotional which uses text and images to draw the reader closer to God. Each week is a step on a journey that begins with the concerns of managing day-to-day life, and ends with a transcendent vision of Heaven.

"Visually captivating and both the words and photography will nourish your soul. If you like *Jesus Calling* you will love this book too."

– JEAN WISE,
AUTHOR OF *FUEL YOUR FAITH*

"Seldom does one find a devotional book in which its depth is matched by its beauty."

— DAVE JACOBS,
AUTHOR OF *MILE WIDE, INCH DEEP*

"For those who have experienced physical, emotional, mental or spiritual pain, this devotional will delight, heal and restore them."

— ARTISAN BOOK REVIEWS

For more information visit

www.messagesfromgoddevotional.com

Messages from God: An Illuminated Devotional and its companion Messages from God: An Illuminated Workbook are both available from Amazon

About the Authors

KATHLEEN SCHWAB is a lifelong lover of God, a literature teacher, a writer, and a wife and mother. She grew up learning about God by reading the popular children's series *The Bible Story*, and devoted her adult life to Jesus at the age of 14. He became her Teacher, Guardian, Companion, and Best Friend. She began speaking in tongues in college, and continues to this day.

In partnership with photographer Therese Kay, Kathleen is the author of *Messages from God: An Illuminated Devotional*, a five-week full color devotional inspired by the illuminated manuscripts of the Middle Ages. Kathleen holds a Bachelor's degree in English Language and Literature, and a Master's degree in Teaching, both from Smith College.

 **MATTHEW SCHWAB** embraced Jesus back when he was a teenager. In college, he began to have unusual experiences that appeared to be spiritual in nature. The teachings of the Reverend Everett "Terry" L. Fullam, the Rector of St. Paul's Episcopal Church in Darien, Connecticut, and a leader in the charismatic movement, helped Matthew to understand what he was experiencing as well as how to enjoy these experiences more deeply.

Today, Matthew is married to Kathleen, is active in the house church movement, and might describe himself as a God-geek, as he wrote his part of this book based upon his studies and experiences. Matthew holds a Bachelor's degree in Economics from Amherst College, and an MBA from the University of Michigan.

 **CHRIS MCKINNEY** built a successful career in investment management after receiving Bachelor's and Master's Degrees in Finance from The University of Alabama. Through a number of divine interventions, Chris was called toward his extraordinary passion for writing, editing, and publishing Christian material. Out of that passion, he founded Called Writers Christian Publishing. Chris is currently an Executive Editor for *GODSPEED Magazine*, where he has the privilege of working under David Aikman, one of the most successful Christian journalists of all-time.

In addition to *GODSPEED*, Chris's articles have been featured by Crosswalk.com, Engage Magazine, Lost Pen Magazine, and several other publications and websites. His first book, *Calling All Writers! — A Small Group Curriculum For Christian Writers* was released in 2018 and is currently available on Amazon. Additionally, Chris has written and edited for several ministries such as The Foundry and Church of the Highlands.

Chris leads teams and small groups at Church of the Highlands, and will soon graduate the ministry training program at Highlands College. He resides in Tuscaloosa, Alabama, with his wife, Shannon, and their three boys.

Notes and References

1 "Global Christianity – A Report on the Size and Distribution of the World's Christian Population." *PewForum*, https://www.pewforum.org/2011/12/19/global-christianity-exec/ Accessed 10 August 2019.

2 Concordia Theological Quarterly, vol 45, #3, July 1981

3 "A Neuroscientific Look at Speaking in Tongues." *NYTimes*, https://www.nytimes.com/2006/11/07/health/07brain.html
Accessed 14 September 2019.

4 This article is not quoted in the book, and was only found by the authors after the passage was written. But it is a great example of a Bible teacher outlining this type of teaching: http://bornofspirit.net/tongues-the-spiritual-gift-vs-tongues-the-prayer-language/

5 "Chuck Smith: Interpretation of Tongues." *Blue Letter Bible*, https://www.blueletterbible.org/Comm/smith_chuck/HolySpirit/hs_24.cfm
Accessed 16 April 2019.

6 "Your Prayer Language And How To Interpret It pt. 1 | Episode 734." *YouTube*, uploaded by Perry Stone, 31 October 2014, https://youtu.be/T_ngo5oVluA?t=779
Relevant comments start at time = 12:59.

7   "Amazing Benefits of Speaking in Tongues! | Janie DuVall."
        YouTube, uploaded by Sid Roth's It's Supernatural!, 4 April
        2018, https://youtu.be/K45vUDb7_wQ
        Relevant comments start at time = 6:00.

8   "Multitasking is scientifically impossible, so give up now."
        The Telegraph, https://www.telegraph.co.uk/women/
        womens-life/11512469/Multitasking-is-scientifically-
        impossible-so-give-up-nowMultitask.html Accessed 18
        July 2019.

9   "What Percentage Of English Words Are Derived From
        Latin?" *Dictionary.com*, https://www.dictionary.com/e/
        word-origins/
        Accessed 1 August 2019.

10   "Alternate forms for the name John." *Wikipedia*, https://
        en.wikipedia.org/wiki/Alternate_forms_for_the_name_
        John
        Accessed 14 September 2019.

11   "What Does It Mean to Bless God?" *DesiringGod* https://
        www.desiringgod.org/articles/what-does-it-mean-to-
        bless-god
        Accessed 18 July 2019.

12   Chris asked for an interpretation that day and this is what
        he believes the Lord gave him. However, Matthew and
        Chris later discussed this topic. Matthew's view, based on 1
        Corinthians 14:2, is that this type of revelation is technically
        not an interpretation of the tongue, but rather a prophetic
        revelation given by God in response to a person's prayer in
        their tongue. Chris, however, believes that in 1 Corinthians
        14:5, Paul puts the tongue-interpretation combination on
        equal ground with prophecy. Ultimately, we decided to
        leave it to readers to study relevant Scripture, ask the Lord
        for understanding, and then draw their own conclusions
        about whether or not a revelation that comes from God's
        perspective can be considered an interpretation, or if it is

simply a prophetic revelation that God gives as a response to a person's prayer in their tongue.

13   John Piper has some excellent teachings on this topic. For those interested in more detail, please see "What Is Prophecy in the New Covenant?" available on YouTube: https://youtu.be/sf1cdXdgFxU and "The New Testament Gift of Prophecy" available on DesiringGod.org: https://www.desiringgod.org/articles/the-new-testament-gift-of-prophecy

D3 - 3,000

Made in the USA
Middletown, DE
12 June 2020